The Blue Ducks'

REAL FOOD

To the ever-growing Three Blue Ducks family and all who continually support us in what we do.

The Blue Ducks'
REAL FOOD

104 DELICIOUS *mostly* WHOLEFOOD RECIPES

MARK LABROOY
& DARREN ROBERTSON

with Hannah Reid

plum.    Pan Macmillan Australia

CONTENTS

Hi there! 7

Thank you! 226

Hi there!

We get asked all the time about our cooking: 'So what sort of food is it?' It's hard to label because there are so many influences – first there's the British influence from Darren and the Sri Lankan influence from Mark. Then there's the melting pot of influences from places we've travelled to all over the world. Winters in Switzerland, summers in Morocco, months in Bali and France. Eating wherever we went and learning how to make a local curry paste or two. Both of us were incubated in fine dining kitchens. Darren worked at Michelin-starred Gravetye Manor in Sussex, England, before moving to Australia, where he met Mark at Tetsuya's in Sydney. Perhaps it was the sunlight hitting the stainless steel cooktop and twinkling into Mark's eye, or maybe it was the heat from the stockpot that Daz was boiling … whatever it was, we became mates. Daz went on to become head chef at Tetsuya's for three years, while Mark moved to Switzerland where he spent 2 years working at Josef, a fine dining restaurant in Zurich.

In 2010, Mark was in Sydney for a holiday, when on a whim, he and two good friends, Sam Reid-Boquist and Chris Sorrell, signed a lease for a cafe in Bronte. Three Blue Ducks was born. About a year later, Jeff Bennett left the pizza shop next door to join the Ducks partnership. Meanwhile, Darren had left Tetsuya's and started The Table Sessions, cooking pop-up dinners in warehouses, parks, cafes and restaurants across Sydney. He hosted a table session at Three Blue Ducks and after dinner service had finished Daz made mention that it had been the most enjoyable table session he'd done. Mark suggested they continue cooking together and Daz came on board as a partner, making five Ducks in total.

When we started The Ducks, we were interested in creating food that was more simple and rough around the edges. We wanted less white tablecloth dining and more just-come-as-you-are. We started sourcing local produce and dressing it up with flavour, proteins and textural elements. The more we experimented with un-doctored food, the more we began to learn about the diverse ways of cooking with different vegetables, grains and legumes to get the most out of them. We started making our own nut butters, milks, cold-pressed juices, oils, salts and vinegars.

We use the kitchen to experiment, and there is always something bubbling or fizzing in there. We attended American food author and activist Sandor Katz's Art of Fermentation talks in Sydney in 2014 and he inspired us with the continued possibilities for ferments in our cooking. When we opened Three Blue Ducks at The Farm in Byron

Bay, we started fermenting as a way of extending the life of produce. We preserve fresh produce to minimise waste from an abundant crop yield. Ferments change your palate as the sourness takes dishes and wakes them up. When you start eating krauts, kimchi, miso, soy and vinegars, food begins to taste a little bit flat without them. Once you dip your toe into the fermenting pool, you find it hard to go back. Now, we have to stop ourselves from putting kimchi and krauts in everything.

So, I guess the food we cook is real food.

Real food has a real beginning – it's planted, grows wild or is born. It is vegetables, fruits, whole grains, seeds, fish and meat. It's food that will eventually rot or perish. It isn't what legendary author of *The Omnivore's Dilemma*, Michael Pollan, calls 'edible food-like substances,' and it isn't made up of ingredients we can't pronounce. Real food is eaten at a table with friends or people you love.

Eating real food is a way of life. While some real food dishes – like fresh salads or stir-fries – are quick and easy to prepare, there others, such as bone broths, slow braises, ferments and nut milks, that take some preparation and time. Today, the average Australian spends about half an hour a day preparing food. We want to bring back the ceremony to our cooking and eating. The fact that we can do fast food so quickly has been established; now let's slow it down and give more attention and time to food preparation and eating, using ingredients that nourish and sustain us.

We never set out to make this book super healthy. We eat well and nutritiously, but also with balance. We cook with sugar and duck fat, we drink coffee and we often have a beer after service. But overall, our food is healthy and nourishing. We are joining a movement that is happening at the moment, led mostly by home cooks, who are showing us that healthy food can be really tasty too. Our food is big, bold and textural. We play with spices, herbs, grains and seeds as a way of engaging with the fresh produce. Chewy spelt and crunchy sesame seeds bring another dimension to a dish that was just a protein and a vegetable.

This is the direction our food is going. We're so much more excited about older techniques of food preparation and cooking than about motion circulators and dry ice. We wanted to create a book based on the sort of cooking we do at home. This book looks at different types of nuts, grains, seeds and spices and how to use them in your cooking. It shows you how to make tasty birdseed for your salads and discusses the differences between cold-pressed and centrifugal juicing. It features Mark's Nana Barney's legendary Love Cake recipe and it demonstrates how to go about creating an epic curry night with all the trimmings. This isn't just a book for chefs; it's a book for people, like us, who want to cook delicious food at home using real ingredients. We love cooking this kind of food and we hope you do too.

Mark and Darren

SALADS
& VEGGIES

CRUNCHY FENNEL AND RED CABBAGE SALAD

This salad is so fresh, it's great with smoked meats and seafood and it goes brilliantly with pork or lamb. For shaved salads like this, I recommend getting your hands on a Japanese mandoline. They're around thirty-five dollars, and they make salads like this so easy. Most professional kitchens have them. They're great for slaws, slicing potatoes for bakes, raw veggie salads, shaving fruits … all sorts. Otherwise, there's nothing wrong with honing your knife skills. It'll just take a bit longer, but it's well worth the effort.

1 fennel bulb (about 200 g), finely sliced
¼ small red cabbage (about 150 g), finely sliced
6 spring onions, white and green parts, finely sliced on an angle
1 granny smith apple, julienned
1 handful of mint leaves, torn
1 handful of flat-leaf parsley leaves, torn
1 tablespoon baby capers in brine
2 tablespoons roasted chopped walnuts

Dressing
1 teaspoon Dijon mustard
1 teaspoon honey
3 tablespoons olive oil
3 tablespoons apple cider vinegar
salt flakes and freshly ground pepper

To make the dressing, combine all the ingredients in a small bowl and season to taste.

Add the fennel, cabbage, spring onion, apple, herbs and capers to a large bowl, pour over the dressing and toss well. Pile into a large serving bowl, sprinkle over the walnuts and serve.

Serves 6 as a side

CHARRED BROCCOLI WITH ALMONDS, LEMON AND CHILLI

For years the only way I cooked broccoli was by boiling it in salted water, refreshing it in iced water and then reheating it to serve alongside the main course as the order was yelled across the kitchen. A lot has changed. I remember listening to chef René Redzepi talk about our relationship to meat and veg and how we tend to focus all our attention on cooking the meat and neglect the vegetables. With meat, we trim it, marinate it, season it, cook it with spices, garlic and olive oil, we baste it, turn it, care for it, rest it and then carve it across the grain, and serve it in its own juices or a well-constructed sauce. With veg, we throw it into a pot of boiling water for two minutes, drain, season and eat. Chefs like René are really changing this by treating veggies as the heroes that they are and experimenting with different ways of cooking them to bring out their best. I often find vegetable dishes can be more exciting than the proteins we usually eat for main course. This recipe is no exception.

2 heads of broccoli
2 tablespoons rice bran oil
salt flakes and freshly
  ground pepper
1 tablespoon slivered almonds
1 tablespoon sesame seeds
1 tablespoon pumpkin seeds
1 long red chilli, finely sliced
1 garlic clove, finely sliced
1 handful of mint leaves
1 handful of coriander leaves
finely grated zest and juice of
  1 small lemon
1 tablespoon olive oil

Preheat the barbecue grill on high or place a chargrill pan over high heat.

Remove the stems from the broccoli heads. Cut away the base of the stem, peel off the skin and cut the stems into 4-mm slices. Cut each head into eight similar-sized pieces so that they cook evenly. Place the broccoli in a large bowl, drizzle over half the rice bran oil and toss to coat. Season the broccoli with salt and grill for 3–4 minutes, turning occasionally. Once cooked, chop the broccoli into florets and add to a large bowl.

Place a dry frying pan over medium heat and toast the almonds and seeds in separate batches until golden.

Gently fry the chilli and garlic in the remaining rice bran oil until the garlic starts turning golden around the edges. Add to the broccoli along with the herbs, almonds, seeds, lemon zest and juice and olive oil. Season, toss to combine and serve.

Serves 6 as a side

FLAVOURED OILS

Making infused oils is dead easy, and they can add an incredible amount of flavour to any salad or veggie dish. Just make sure you only use quality oil and produce to ensure that you get the best tasting oil.

Lemon, thyme and garlic oil

This is a very versatile oil that can add a punch of citrus and herb to chicken, meat, fish or vegetables.

800 ml grapeseed oil
1 lemon, sliced
8 garlic cloves
½ bunch of thyme

For this recipe, you will need a sterilised 1-litre glass bottle with a lid (see page 155 for instructions on sterilising).

Add the oil to a medium saucepan over low heat – you don't want to heat it up too much, but enough to extract flavour from the aromatics.

Add the lemon, garlic and thyme to the bottle. Tip the warm oil into a pouring jug and pour it into the bottle, being careful as the oil will be pretty warm.

After a few days, the flavour will have really developed and it will be ready to use.

Makes 800 ml

Chilli, lemongrass and ginger oil

I really like using this one on chargrilled octopus or crispy skinned barramundi or mulloway. It's also awesome with kingfish ceviche. Don't like it too hot? Then scrape out some of the chilli seeds, but not all of them, or it won't have any heat at all.

800 ml grapeseed oil
4 long red chillies, split lengthways
70 g young ginger, peeled and cut to fit in the bottle
1 lemongrass stem, base bruised and the top trimmed to just fit in the bottle

For this recipe, you will need a sterilised 1-litre glass bottle with a lid (see page 155 for instructions on sterilising).

Add the oil to a medium saucepan over low–medium heat and warm for a couple of minutes – you don't want to heat it up too much, but enough to extract flavour from the aromatics.

Add the chilli and ginger to the bottle. Tip the warm oil into a pouring jug and pour it into the bottle, being careful, as the oil will be quite warm. Place the lemongrass in the bottle and set aside to cool.

After a few days, the flavour will have really developed and it will be ready to use.

Makes 800 ml

CHARRED BROAD BEAN AND POTATO SALAD

Potato salad is probably seen as a bit of a daggy dish. But it doesn't mean you can't bring it to life. When broad beans are in season they're a great addition, as is shaved raw celeriac, shredded cabbage, snow peas, garlic flowers or torn radicchio. Try not to make this hours in advance, though – a potato salad that's just been made, even still warm, simply dressed in mayonnaise with cornichons, capers and freshly picked herbs can be a thing of beauty. So many things taste better at a gentle room temperature and don't benefit from being served straight from the refrigerator.

1 kg kipfler potatoes,
  scrubbed and cut in half
  (or left whole if small)
500 g broad beans in
  their pods
1 tablespoon rice bran oil
3 tablespoons chopped
  cornichons
2 tablespoons baby capers
  in brine
2 spring onions, white and
  green parts, finely sliced
1 handful of flat-leaf parsley
  leaves, chopped
salt flakes and freshly
  ground pepper

Lemon mayonnaise
1 egg yolk
1 tablespoon Dijon mustard
½ tablespoon white
  wine vinegar
½ teaspoon soy sauce
finely grated zest and
  juice of 1 lemon
50 ml olive oil
200 ml rice bran oil
salt flakes and freshly
  ground pepper

Preheat the barbecue grill on high or place a chargrill pan over high heat.

Add the potatoes to a saucepan of cold salted water and bring to the boil. Simmer for 15–20 minutes until cooked. Drain well and set aside to cool in a serving bowl.

Meanwhile, coat the broad bean pods in rice bran oil and grill until almost black on both sides. Set the pods aside to cool.

To make the mayonnaise, add the yolk, mustard, vinegar, soy and lemon zest and juice to a medium bowl and whisk until combined. Slowly pour in both oils while whisking constantly – pour very slowly at first, making sure that the mix emulsifies, and then speed up the process as the mayonnaise becomes more stable. This should take 3–4 minutes of constant whisking to make. Season to taste.

Remove the cooled broad beans from their pods and add to the potatoes. Add most of the mayonnaise, the cornichons, capers, spring onion and parsley to the bowl and mix until combined. Add a little more of the mayonnaise if you like, adjust the seasoning to taste and serve.

Any leftover mayonnaise will keep in an airtight container in the fridge for 3–4 days.

Serves 4–6

HAM HOCK, RADISH AND PEAR SALAD

Slowly cooking a ham hock will give you many meals with little effort. Keep hold of the cooking liquid, as it's full of flavour. Add some frozen peas, cook for a minute or two and then blend for pea and ham soup. Or add cooked chickpeas, smoked paprika and kale for something heartier. This salad should be wet, punchy, sweet, smoky and acidic. For a bit more kick, use English mustard instead of Dijon, and if you don't have any pears, apples work just as well.

1 smoked ham hock
1 onion, quartered
2 celery stalks, cut in half
3 garlic cloves, bruised
6 black peppercorns
5 small red radishes
1 firm packham pear
1 small red onion
1 handful of watercress
1 handful of flat-leaf
   parsley leaves
¼ cup roasted hazelnuts,
   roughly chopped
salt flakes and freshly
   ground pepper

Dressing
finely grated zest and juice
   of ½ lemon
3 tablespoons olive oil
2 tablespoons cider vinegar
2 teaspoons seeded mustard
2 teaspoons Dijon mustard
2 teaspoons honey

Place the ham hock in a medium saucepan with the onion, celery, garlic, peppercorns and enough water to cover (about 2½ litres). Bring to the boil, then reduce the heat and skim off any scum that has come to the surface. Simmer for about 1½ hours, or until the meat begins to come away from the bone. Take off the heat and set aside to cool in the liquid.

Once cool enough to handle, pick the meat from the bones, discarding the skin and any gristle. Break the meat down into bite-sized pieces and add to a large bowl. Strain the stock and refrigerate or freeze for later use.

To make the dressing, place all the ingredients in a small bowl and whisk until combined. Pour the dressing over the meat and mix well.

Using a mandoline or sharp knife, shave the radishes, pear and red onion finely. Add to the dressed hock meat with the watercress, parsley and hazelnuts. Toss gently, adjust the seasoning if necessary and serve.

Serves 4

RAW VEGGIE SALAD WITH BIRDSEED AND POMEGRANATE

A raw veggie salad is such an easy and tasty way to introduce raw vegetables into your diet on a daily basis. Eating raw vegetables means that you're receiving the full nutrient potential of that vegetable, as nothing is lost through the cooking process. Needless to say, selecting seasonal organic produce is ideal for this, but don't be too worried about following the recipe to the letter, use anything you like from your crisper.

¼ iceberg lettuce, finely shredded
¼ small red cabbage, finely shredded
1 large beetroot, julienned
½ zucchini, finely sliced
½ red onion, finely sliced
½ granny smith apple, julienned
3 radishes, finely sliced
1 handful of snow peas, strings removed, sliced in half lengthways
1 handful of flat-leaf parsley, leaves picked and roughly chopped
1 pomegranate, cut in half
salt flakes and freshly ground pepper
4 tablespoons birdseed mix (chia seeds, poppy seeds, pumpkin seeds, sunflower seeds, sesame seeds, flaxseeds or whatever you have in the pantry)
2 tablespoons roughly chopped salted cashews

Lemon dressing
75 ml good-quality olive oil
2 teaspoons honey
1 teaspoon Dijon mustard
finely grated zest of 1 lemon and juice of 2 lemons
salt flakes and freshly ground pepper

To make the lemon dressing, combine all the ingredients in a small bowl and season to taste.

Add the lettuce, cabbage, beetroot, zucchini, onion, apple, radish, snow peas and parsley to a large bowl. Add the lemon dressing to taste and, using your hands, carefully toss.

Hit the back of each pomegranate half with a wooden spoon so that the juicy seeds pop out onto the salad. Season and gently toss.

Transfer the salad to a serving bowl and sprinkle the seed mix and cashews over the top before serving.

Serves 4

FLAVOURED SALTS

Making your own salts is one of the easiest ways to introduce flavour to your food. Be it a piece of grilled fish, a steak, or a tray of oven-roasted vegetables, a flavoured salt will make all the difference. Whenever I make a batch of salt, I leave a little jar near the stovetop so that I remember to use it. Also see page 27 for fennel salt and page 167 for tea-smoked salt.

Thyme, lemon and fennel salt

Citrus salt (see Flavoured salt, your way)

Five-spice salt

Mixed pepper salt

Five-spice salt

This is great with any kind of pork dish, or sprinkled on fish fillets before pan-frying.

8 cloves
3 star anise
3 teaspoons Sichuan peppercorns
2 teaspoons fennel seeds
100 g salt flakes
2 teaspoons ground cinnamon

Toast the cloves, star anise, peppercorns and fennel seeds in a dry frying pan over medium heat until fragrant and lightly coloured. Using a mortar and pestle, grind the spices to a powder. Add the salt and cinnamon and mix well with a spoon, keeping the salt flakes nice and large. Store in a dry glass jar.

Makes about 1 cup

Mixed pepper salt

Beef in peppercorn sauce is an absolute classic. Back in the day, certainly in my hometown, everyone had beef fillet on the menu and it was usually served with a pepper sauce, veggies and mashed potato or rosti. These days, other cuts of meat have become more commonplace, but beef and pepper are as good friends as ever. This salt will transform seafood, roasted vegetables or any cut of steak into something amazing.

1 tablespoon black peppercorns
1 tablespoon white peppercorns
2 tablespoons pink peppercorns
1 tablespoon dried pepperberries
100 g salt flakes

Using a mortar and pestle, smash the peppercorns and pepperberries to a rough powder. Add the salt flakes and mix well with a spoon, keeping the salt flakes nice and large. Store in a dry glass jar. You can also mix all the peppers with rock salt in a bowl then add to a pepper grinder for an instant salt and pepper seasoning.

Makes about 1 cup

Thyme, lemon and fennel salt

This is a super versatile salt that can be used on chicken, fish, meat or vegetables. It's also a great way to add a little citrus and herb punch when you don't have the fresh stuff to hand.

1 teaspoon fennel seeds
1 teaspoon coriander seeds
100 g salt flakes
2 teaspoons chopped thyme leaves
finely grated zest of 1 lemon

Toast the fennel and coriander seeds in a dry frying pan over medium heat until fragrant and lightly coloured. Using a mortar and pestle, grind the spices to a powder. Add the salt, thyme and lemon zest and mix well with a spoon, keeping the salt flakes nice and large. Store in a dry glass jar.

Makes about 1 cup

Flavoured salt, your way

There are no measurements here; simply choose from the ingredients below. Olive and basil salt is lovely with bread and butter, chilli salted fries are amazing, and using citrus salt around the rim of a margarita is next level. You'll need a dehydrator for these.

chillies, deseeded
pitted olives
basil leaves (or any herbs that you love)
orange peel, pith removed (or any citrus peel)
salt flakes

Arrange the flavouring ingredients on dehydrator trays and dry on medium for 6–12 hours or until shriveled and wrinkly (herbs will take much less time to dry than other ingredients). Using a mortar and pestle, crush the ingredients separately – don't crush them too much or you'll turn them to powder. Start by mixing equal parts salt to flavouring, and then adjust to taste. Store in dry glass jars.

THE BEST GREEN SALAD

This is a stunning little summer salad, and dead easy to prepare. If you don't have any plum vinegar to hand, apple cider, white wine or sherry vinegar will all work well. Alternatively, squeeze in an orange or lemon. If your leaves are beginning to wilt in the fridge (which happens to us all) simply fill a big bowl with iced water and submerge the leaves for 10 minutes; they should spring right back to life. And, if you don't already own one, invest in a salad spinner. It's the best way to properly dry your salad.

2 tablespoons pumpkin seeds
1 handful of watercress
2 handfuls of rocket
1 handful of mint leaves
1 handful of chervil
1 handful of sorrel
1 handful of snow peas,
** finely sliced**
1 tablespoon poppy seeds

Dressing
2 tablespoons umeboshi
** vinegar (Japanese plum**
** vinegar)**
2½ tablespoons olive oil
1 pinch of chilli flakes
salt flakes and freshly
** ground pepper**

Toast the pumpkin seeds in a dry frying pan for 2–3 minutes until slightly golden. Set aside to cool.

Rinse all the leaves and herbs in ice-cold water, dry in a salad spinner and place in a large bowl with the snow peas.

To make the dressing, combine all the ingredients in a small bowl.

When ready to serve, add the poppy and pumpkin seeds to the salad, pour over the dressing, toss and serve.

Serves 4

BAKED ARTICHOKES WITH GOAT'S CHEESE AND WALNUTS

This is a handy technique for cooking seafood or veggies; it's perfect for a barbecue and there's no washing up. It also works just as well in the oven for those who don't have a barbie. If you want to get a bit fancy, once cooked, carefully open the bag, sprinkle the nuts and cheese on top and pop it back in the oven, uncovered, to roast the nuts and melt the cheese. Squeeze over a touch of lemon and serve.

8 small new potatoes
8 Jerusalem artichokes,
   scrubbed
4 garlic cloves, skin on
1 tablespoon olive oil
1 knob of butter
finely grated zest of
   ½ lemon
4 thyme sprigs
salt flakes and freshly
   ground pepper
60 g goat's cheese
1 small handful of walnuts,
   roughly broken

Preheat the oven to 180°C fan-forced (200°C conventional).

Place an A4-sized piece of baking paper on top of a double layer of foil that's long enough to wrap the vegetables in. Place the potatoes, artichokes and garlic in the middle of the baking paper and top with the olive oil, butter, lemon zest and thyme, season and wrap to make a sealed parcel. Place on a baking tray and bake for 40 minutes.

Carefully open the parcel, squeeze over a little lemon juice from the zested lemon and scatter over the goat's cheese and walnuts. Leave to cool a little before serving.

Serves 4

CARROT AND BEETROOT CRUMBS WITH FENNEL SALT

This really is a great way to use up the remnants of juiced carrots and beetroots from your morning juice. Some of the best recipes at the Ducks have come about through finding ways to use up by-products. Solving a problem is always a great motivation for creativity. You can go down the sweet road with this, just leave out the fennel salt and add to granola, muffins, cakes, chocolate brownies or ice cream. Or go to savoury town and add to pies, yoghurt, dips and salads – anywhere but the bin.

350 g carrot pulp
350 g beetroot pulp
2 teaspoons olive oil

Fennel salt
1 teaspoon fennel seeds
⅓ cup salt flakes

To make the fennel salt, toast the fennel seeds in a dry frying pan until fragrant and lightly coloured.

Using a mortar and pestle, crush the seeds to a coarse powder. Add the salt and combine, crushing a little but still keeping some texture in the flakes. You will have more salt than is needed for this recipe, so store the remainder in a dry glass jar. Use it to season steaks, seafood or salads.

Mix the vegetable pulp with the oil and season with a good pinch of fennel salt. Spread out on dehydrator trays in layers about 4–5-mm thick and dry on medium for about 10 hours. This will keep for 2–3 months in a sealed jar.

You can also use whole vegetables for this, just whizz in a food processor until pulpy and place in the dehydrator trays as described – the pulp will have a lot more juice in it and will take closer to 24 hours to dehydrate, but it will also be a lot sweeter and more intensely flavoured.

Makes 3 cups

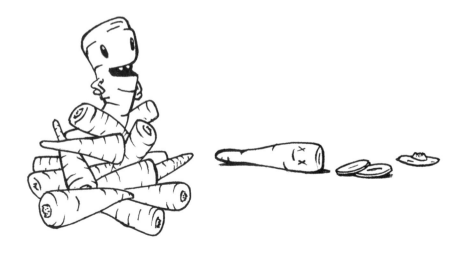

SPICY THAI BEEF SALAD

We've served this salad at many of our pop-up events. Without the beef, it's a fantastic vegetarian option, or for the more carnivorous eater, use beef or even crispy-skinned duck breast. It's perfect after a hot summer's day with a glass of riesling. If you feel like it, sprinkle with roasted cashews and salted fried shallots.

4 × 220 g sirloin steaks
rice bran oil, to grill
salt flakes and freshly
　ground pepper
250 g cherry tomatoes,
　quartered
1 red onion, finely sliced
5 spring onions, green part only,
　finely sliced
½ green mango, peeled and
　shaved with a vegetable peeler
200 g baby corn, each cob
　sliced on an angle into thirds
1 punnet enoki mushrooms,
　base trimmed and stems
　broken up
2 handfuls of snow peas,
　strings removed, sliced in
　half lengthways
2 handfuls of bean sprouts
4 handfuls of baby kale, torn into
　bite-sized pieces
1 large bunch of coriander,
　leaves picked and roughly
　chopped, roots reserved for
　the dressing
2 handfuls of mint, leaves
　picked and roughly chopped
1 handful of Thai basil leaves, torn

Dressing
125 g cherry tomatoes
2 long red chillies, roughly
　chopped
2 garlic cloves
60 g ginger, finely grated
1 bunch of coriander roots
　(from above), roughly chopped
50 g palm sugar
45 ml fish sauce
1 teaspoon soy sauce, plus extra
juice of 4 limes
juice of 2 lemons

Preheat the barbecue grill on high.

For the dressing, add everything except for the citrus juice to a mortar and grind until a smooth paste. Add the citrus juice, stir and taste. Add a little more soy sauce if it's not salty enough.

Rub the steaks with oil and season. Grill until just medium–rare, about 3–4 minutes each side. Be sure not to overcook the steaks, it's better to keep them on the rare side, as the acidity of the dressing will cook the meat further. Rest the steaks for about 10 minutes. Slice thinly and then toss back into the juices on the resting tray.

Add the remaining ingredients to a large bowl and combine. Toss the sliced beef through the salad, add all of the dressing, toss again and serve.

Serves 4–6

7. OATS

A grain we are all familiar with, oats are warm and soothing. They begin as hulled oat kernels called oat groats and are then either steel-cut into smaller pieces, rolled by being flattened under high pressure, or milled into flour.

To cook steel-cut oats: Bring 1 cup of oats and 3–4 cups of water or milk to the boil in a medium saucepan. Reduce the heat, cover and simmer for 20–30 minutes until the oats are creamy.

Ideas for using oats:
- Use steel-cut oats in porridge.
- Use raw oats in muesli.
- Use oats in cookie dough.

8. QUINOA

An ancient grain cultivated in the Andes, quinoa was traditionally the peasant food of the Inca. Technically a seed rather than a grain, quinoa is available in many colours, including red, brown and white. Always rinse quinoa well, it has a natural coating of saponin, which the plant produces to deter insects and birds, and can leave the cooked grain tasting bitter or soapy.

To cook quinoa by the absorption method: Rinse and drain the quinoa. Bring 1 cup of quinoa and 2 cups of water or broth to the boil in a medium saucepan. Reduce the heat, cover tightly and simmer for 10–20 minutes until all the water has been absorbed. Remove from the heat and cool. Stir through some butter or olive oil and season to taste.

Ideas for using quinoa:
- Add it to any and all salads.
- Throw raw quinoa into soups as they cook.
- Add it to muffins for extra protein.

9. RICE: WILD AND BROWN

Brown rice is whole grain rice that has only had its outer hull removed. Brown rice is starchy and chewy.

Wild rice is not technically rice but actually a grass seed, which also means that it's gluten-free. Wild rice has almost twice the amount of fibre per serving as brown rice. It's crunchier than brown rice and has a distinct earthy flavour.

To cook brown and wild rice: Rinse and drain the rice. Bring 1 cup of rice and 4 cups of water or broth to the boil in a medium saucepan. Reduce the heat, cover and simmer for 45 minutes or until cooked through. Remove from the heat and strain off any liquid. Fluff the rice with a fork and season to taste.

Ideas for using brown or wild rice:
- Use brown or wild rice in a pilaf.
- Add brown or wild rice to soups.
- Fry cooked brown or wild rice with pork, cabbage and spiced apple.
- Use as the base for chicken stuffing.

10. RYE

Rye was long considered a weed in wheat crops, until farmers started to take note of its hardiness and ability to withstand drought and flooding. Often referred to as the poverty grain, rye thrives in soils that are too poor for other grains. It is typically used in breads and crispbreads, and has a sour, tangy taste. You can buy rye as flour, whole grain rye kernels or as rolled rye flakes.

To cook whole grain rye by the absorption method: Soak the rye kernels overnight. Rinse and drain the rye. Bring 3 cups of water to the boil in a medium saucepan and add 1 cup of rye. Return to the boil and simmer for 45 minutes. The kernels should be cooked through but still firm and chewy. Fluff the rye with a fork and season to taste.

Ideas for using whole grain rye:
- Add it to soups.
- Add it to vegetable stir-fries.
- Mix with rice and serve with curries.

11. SPELT

A species of wheat, spelt is rich, sweet, nutty and chewy. You can buy spelt as whole grain kernels or flour. Spelt is not gluten-free, though it does have significantly lower levels of gluten than wheat.

To cook spelt: If you want the spelt kernels soft, like steamed rice, bring 1 cup of spelt and 3 cups of water or broth to the boil in a medium saucepan. Reduce the heat, cover tightly and simmer for 1–1½ hours. If you want the spelt to be chewier, use 1 cup of spelt and 2 cups of water, cook it like risotto, adding half a cup of liquid at a time and stirring until the liquid is absorbed. The spelt should be cooked after about 30–40 minutes.

Ideas for using spelt:
- Use spelt instead of rice in a risotto.
- Add cooked spelt kernels to salads.
- Use spelt flour in your pizza dough for a sweeter, earthier flavour.

12. TEFF

The staple grain of Ethiopia, teff consists mostly of the bran and germ, making it incredibly nutritious. It tastes smooth and mild with a slightly gelatinous texture akin to polenta. Teff is often ground into flour but is just as delicious as a whole grain.

To cook teff by the absorption method: Toast 1 cup of teff in a frying pan. Bring the teff and 3 cups of water to the boil in a medium saucepan. Reduce the heat, cover and simmer for 15–20 minutes. The water should be absorbed and the teff should be creamy. Fluff the teff with a fork, and season to taste.

Ideas for using teff:
- Add to veggie patties.
- Toss cooled teff through salads.
- Mix teff flour with wholemeal flour to make bread dough.

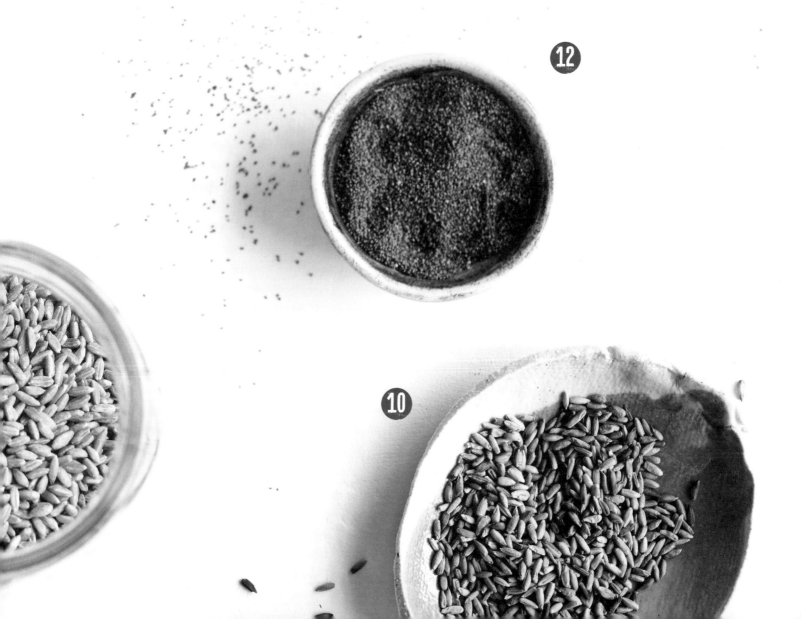

CARROT, GINGER AND RHUBARB PORRIDGE

I enjoy porridge, but it does have a reputation for being a bit bland and boring. This recipe incorporates a variety of grains and no refined sugars. It's definitely a far cry from the traditional formula of stodgy oats and plenty of brown sugar. If you're lactose intolerant, use a coconut-based yoghurt instead of regular yoghurt. This porridge will definitely keep you going until lunchtime.

4 rhubarb stalks, cut into
   5-cm lengths
1 tablespoon raw sugar
6 carrots, juiced
10-cm piece of ginger, juiced
50 g buckwheat groats
50 g pearl barley
50 g wild rice (or red rice)
50 g couscous
50 g quinoa
60 g rolled oats
1 teaspoon salt flakes
1 tablespoon honey
natural yoghurt, to serve
honeycomb, to serve
   (optional)

Seed mix
2 tablespoons shredded
   coconut
2 tablespoons chia seed
1 tablespoon flaxseeds
1 tablespoon sesame seeds

Preheat the oven to 180°C fan-forced (200°C conventional).

Place the rhubarb on a lined baking tray. Sprinkle with the sugar and bake for 25 minutes.

Meanwhile, combine all the ingredients for the seed mix in a small bowl and set aside.

Place a medium saucepan over medium–high heat. Add the carrot and ginger juices, buckwheat, barley, wild rice, couscous, quinoa, oats and salt and cook, stirring frequently, for about 25 minutes. The mix will become thick and creamy. Stir continually once it thickens to stop it catching.

Meanwhile, add the cooked rhubarb to a blender and blitz to a smooth puree.

To serve, stir the honey through the porridge and spoon into bowls. Top with a good spoonful of yoghurt, some rhubarb puree and a piece of honeycomb (if using). Sprinkle over some seed mix and serve.

Serves 6

APPLE BIRCHER WITH CHIA AND ROASTED NUTS

I learnt how to make bircher muesli while living in Zurich, Switzerland. It's a staple over there, something that you just have to know how to make before you move out of home. It's a simple dish, and tasty to boot. If you can get your hands on freshly rolled oats then it will be next level. Add whatever fruits you like, just try to stay seasonal.

500 g rolled oats
500 ml fresh apple juice
500 g natural yoghurt
1 apple, grated
1 pear, grated
60 g chia seeds
150 g roasted almonds,
　roughly chopped
125 g roughly chopped
　walnuts (or hazelnuts)
1 handful of strawberries
1 handful of blueberries
75 g currants
honey, to serve

Mix the oats and apple juice in a medium bowl and refrigerate overnight.

In the morning, fold in the yoghurt, apple and pear. It should be quite a moist and creamy mix, if it seems a bit stodgy, add some more yoghurt. Be careful not to mix it too much, as the gluten in the oats will start to develop and it will become glue-like.

Spoon a good dollop of the bircher into breakfast bowls, sprinkle over some chia seeds and nuts, followed by the berries and currants and a good drizzle of honey.

Serves 6

MAGDALENA'S PUMPKIN BREAD

This recipe is from my missus, Magdalena Roze. Don't be put off by the list of ingredients, it's actually really easy and so full of nourishing flavour. If you're looking for a more savoury bread, just use olive oil instead of macadamia, or if you're after something a little sweeter, add some chopped dates. I usually toast a couple of slices after a surf, and eat them with a handful of blueberries and some ricotta. But it's also very tasty with sliced tomato, avocado and basil. The nuts and seeds are optional (and feel free to mix and match) but I like it crunchy and chunky.

3 cups grated raw pumpkin

3 eggs

1 tablespoon honey

2 tablespoons macadamia oil

1 generous pinch of salt flakes

½ teaspoon ground nutmeg

½ teaspoon ground cinnamon

2 cups almond meal

½ cup coconut flour

squeeze of lemon juice

⅔ teaspoon bicarbonate of soda

⅔ cup chopped pecans (optional)

4 tablespoons chia seeds (optional)

4 tablespoons sunflower seeds, plus extra (optional)

4 tablespoons pumpkin seeds (optional)

Preheat the oven to 160°C fan-forced (180°C conventional). Grease a 25-cm loaf tin and line with baking paper.

Combine the pumpkin, eggs, honey and oil in a large bowl. Add the salt, nutmeg and cinnamon and combine. Mix in the almond meal, coconut flour, lemon juice and bicarbonate of soda. If the mix feels too wet, add a little more coconut flour. Add the pecans and seeds (if using) and gently fold through until combined.

Tip the mixture into the prepared tin, sprinkle the top with extra sunflower seeds and bake for 1–1½ hours until a skewer comes out clean. Tip out of the tin and cool before slicing and serving.

Serves 10–12

How to make
ALMOND MILK

It seems that almond milk is all the rage at the moment. In fact, techniques for making nut milk have been employed since the Dark Ages and the method, aside from the blender, hasn't changed much in all that time. To make the most of the process, it's important to take the time to activate the almonds first. Simply put, this involves soaking the almonds overnight to stop the phytic acid from restricting the full benefit of the nut from being processed by the body. This soaking period deactivates the enzyme inhibitors and unlocks the full nutritional potential of the nut. You can make larger quantities if you like – just keep the same ratio of almonds to water. For this recipe, you will need a nut milk bag (about $15 on the internet) or some muslin or cheesecloth.

You'll need:
    500 g raw almonds
    1 pinch of salt flakes
    1 litre purified water

Makes 1.25 litres

Take the soaked almonds from the refrigerator and drain off the water. The water will be cloudy and viscous. Discard this or pour it straight on the garden.

Put the almonds in a large jar or bowl, cover with tap or filtered water and stir in the salt. Place the jar in the refrigerator overnight or for 7–10 hours.

Place the almonds in a blender, add the purified water and blend thoroughly.

The nuts will blend into the liquid and the mix will be thick and rich.

Pour the contents of the blender into a nut milk bag or some muslin or cheesecloth over a large container or food-suitable bucket.

Squeeze the liquid from the bag so that the nutty, creamy milk fills the container. Keep squeezing until you can't extract any more liquid, and the almond meal starts to feel dry to the touch.

Stir the almond milk well and pour into bottles or glass jars. Drink within 2–3 days.

Be sure to keep the almond meal, as you can use this for making cakes, protein balls and pastry bases. Store it in an airtight container in the fridge and use within 3–4 days.

MIXED GRAIN SALAD

The beauty of a mixed grain salad is that you can use whatever grains you have to hand: quinoa, amaranth, pearl barley, Israeli couscous or even wild rice. Mixed with some red cabbage, parsley and onion, this simple salad definitely becomes a meal, but it also makes a great side with grilled lamb chops and yoghurt dressing, or crispy-skinned fish with some salsa verde (see page 148).

100 g amaranth
100 g Israeli couscous
100 g pearl barley
100 g quinoa
75 g currants
¼ red cabbage, finely sliced
1 large handful of flat-leaf parsley, leaves picked and finely chopped
1 red onion, finely sliced
salt flakes and freshly ground pepper
1 quantity Lemon Dressing (see page 20)

Simmer each of the grains separately until al dente. You can cook these in four small or medium saucepans at the same time, just watch for different cooking times. Drain well, combine in a large bowl and set aside to cool.

Add the currants, cabbage, parsley and onion to the cooled grains, season and combine. Add the dressing to taste, toss well and serve.

Serves 6 as a side

MIXED GRAIN 'RISOTTO' WITH BACON AND PEAS

This style of 'risotto' goes really well with a grilled piece of barramundi or crispy-skinned jewfish. You can also serve it with steamed vegetables, or roasted brussels sprouts or root vegetables. We created this dish when we wanted something lighter than the traditionally heavy, creamy and cheesy risotto that we're all familiar with.

100 g pearl barley
100 g Israeli couscous
100 g red quinoa
100 g Puy lentils
3 tablespoons vegetable oil
1 large red onion, finely diced
3 garlic cloves, finely chopped
4 rashers of bacon, cut into
   lardons
2 long red chillies, deseeded
   and julienned
300 ml vegetable stock
50 g butter
250 g frozen peas
1 large handful of mint, leaves
   picked and torn
salt flakes and freshly ground
   pepper
juice of ½ lemon

Simmer the barley, couscous, quinoa and lentils separately until al dente. You can cook these in four small or medium saucepans at the same time, just watch for different cooking times. Drain well, combine and set aside.

Heat a medium, heavy-based saucepan over high heat. Add the oil, onion, garlic, bacon and chilli and cook until the onions are soft and the bacon starts to caramelise. Add the grains and 250 ml of stock and stir gently for 3–4 minutes. The starches in the grains will start to thicken up the liquid, keep cooking until you have a risotto-like consistency. Add the butter and, once melted, add the peas and mint, squeeze over the lemon juice and season to taste. If it looks a little dry, add some more stock. Spoon into bowls and serve.

Serves 4 as a side

SPELT SALAD WITH RADICCHIO AND PINK GRAPEFRUIT

The sour grapefruit and the slightly bitter radicchio work really well with something sweet and rich, like slow-roasted pork shoulder. If you're enjoying it as a standalone salad and it's too bitter for your taste, add a little more honey to the dressing or crumble in some goat's cheese.

150 g spelt
2 heads of radicchio
1 pink grapefruit
80 ml olive oil
1 teaspoon honey
salt flakes and freshly
    ground pepper
3 tablespoons chopped
    roasted macadamias
1 large handful of flat-leaf
    parsley, leaves picked
1 large handful of mint,
    leaves picked
1 tablespoon chia seeds

Cook the spelt in boiling salted water for 50 minutes. Drain, refresh in iced water and drain again.

Separate the radicchio leaves and rinse in cold water. Dry thoroughly before roughly tearing into a large bowl.

Peel and segment the grapefruit. Cut the segments into three pieces each and add to the bowl with the radicchio. Squeeze the juice from the grapefruit membrane into a small bowl. Add the olive oil and honey to the juice, season and combine.

Add the spelt, macadamias, parsley, mint and chia to the radicchio, pour over the dressing and toss well. Adjust the seasoning if necessary, pile into a large bowl and serve.

Serves 4–6

THE AMAZING BENEFITS OF USING NUTS AND SEEDS IN YOUR COOKING

DARREN: My first memory of eating nuts was at home over Christmas. Mum would always have a huge bowl and a nutcracker on the table for anyone who stopped by. It would sit there for the entire duration of Christmas, with a few extra nuts kept aside to fill our stockings. The hazelnuts and walnuts would be the first to go, and the Brazil nuts always the last – they're pretty bloody tough to open, especially when you're a kid.

Edible nuts and seeds have long been an essential part of the human diet. In fact, archaeologists at the Gesher Benot Ya'aqov site in Israel's Hula Valley found the remains of edible nuts and nutcrackers that were over 780,000 years old. What was an annual tradition for my family was a way of life for prehistoric hunter-gatherers who relied on edible nuts and seeds as a key food source.

The inventory of health benefits associated with eating seeds and nuts is encyclopedic. Incredibly nutrient-dense, nuts and seeds are loaded with essential vitamins, minerals, fats, protein, and fibre. To fully experience their potential, buy raw nuts that are not toasted or roasted and store them in an airtight container in the fridge for a few months, or in the freezer for up to a year.

However, like grains and legumes, nuts and seeds contain phytic acid and enzyme inhibitors that are hard to digest and that reduce our body's ability to absorb nutrients. Activating them starts the process of germination or sprouting, which makes them bioactive, maximizing the nutrients available to us. It can also help reduce the amount of pesticides on them if they are not organically grown.

To activate, first create a salty brine to deactivate the enzyme inhibitors. Dissolve 2 tablespoons of salt in enough water to cover the nuts (or seeds). Add 3 cups of nuts to a bowl and cover with the brine. Soak overnight or for around 7–10 hours (if you are activating cashews or macadamias only soak them for 3–6 hours or they will become slimy). Strain and rinse the nuts and then spread out on a baking tray. Dry in the oven on the lowest possible temperature for 12–24 hours – food dehydrators are quite cheap to buy and will free up your oven, plus they have so many other uses. Make sure the nuts have dried completely before storing them or they will be prone to mould.

The health benefits of nuts and seeds are one incentive to cook with them, but the textural element is what really spurs me towards experimenting with them.

MARK: As a kid, my favourite treat was the sesame snap. I spent my whole childhood eating them. I remember the day Klaus, my first ever chef when I was an apprentice, roasted off hazelnuts, sesame seeds, pistachios, cashews and Brazil nuts and poured caramel over them to create an industrial-sized nut snap. I officially lost my mind. There is so much you can do with seeds and nuts beyond regular trail mix. Adding mixed nuts or toasted seeds to a dish lights it up texturally and gives it incredible complexity.

1. ALMONDS

An incredibly versatile nut, almonds are available in many forms: raw, roasted, slivered, sliced, as meal and also as milk.

Ideas for using almonds:
- Cover raw almonds in tamari and roast them for a tasty snack.
- Chop finely and sprinkle over soups and curries.
- Add to braises and tagines.
- Make your own almond milk (see page 52).
- Use in carrot top pesto (see page 193).

2. CASHEWS

Originally native to Brazil, cashews are now grown internationally. High levels of starch make cashews very effective in thickening water-based dishes like curries and soups.

Ideas for using cashews:
- Use in pesto instead of pine nuts.
- Make cashew butter (see page 68) and spread on toast with a drizzle of honey.
- Add to stir-fries and curries (see page 90).
- Use in seed and nut snaps (see page 76).

3. CHIA SEEDS

Chia seeds come from *Salvia hispanica*, a desert plant native to Mexico, and were used by Aztec and Mayan cultures to sustain energy. Chia seeds are full of anti-inflammatory antioxidants and omega-3 fats, and they contain five times more calcium than milk.

Experiment with mixing your chia seeds with liquids like water, raw juice or milk and see the gelatinous, tapioca-like pudding that forms.

Ideas for using chia seeds:
- Add them to muesli, muffins and smoothies (see page 224), or sprinkle over salads.
- Make a chia seed pudding by mixing chia seeds with coconut water and berries and soaking overnight (see page 196).
- Add to protein balls (see page 78).

4. FLAXSEEDS

Otherwise known as linseeds, flaxseeds are a rich source of fibre and omega-3 fatty acids. Flaxseeds are available in two varieties: brown and golden. They are best purchased whole and ground at home as they go rancid quickly once ground.

Ideas for using flaxseeds:
- Add ground flaxseeds to smoothies or muesli for a nutritional boost.
- Grind to create a crust to top banana breads and other cakes.
- Sprinkle over salads.
- Make sesame and flaxseed crackers (see page 74).

5. HEMP SEEDS

The hulled hemp seed is soft and has a flavour similar to a pine nut. Hemp seeds contain all the essential amino acids, making them a complete protein source.

Ideas for using hemp seeds:
- Add to smoothies for a protein hit.
- Sprinkle over salads.

6. MACADAMIA NUTS

Rich and oily in flavour, macadamia nuts are native to Australia. Although they have an incredibly high fat content, it is mainly monounsaturated fat, which reduces bad cholesterol levels in the blood and can lower the risk of heart disease.

Ideas for using macadamia nuts:
- Raw macadamias make a great snack on their own.
- Grind into macadamia nut butter (see page 68).
- Grind lightly and add to pastry dough or tart bases for a great textural element.

7. PEANUTS

Grown underground, peanuts are actually legumes. Eat them raw or roasted. A spoonful of raw peanut butter is great on porridge or in a morning smoothie.

Ideas for using peanuts:
- Grind to make your own raw peanut butter (see page 68).
- Use them in nut and seed bars (see page 75).

8. PISTACHIOS

Pistachios are a member of the cashew family and were originally cultivated in the Middle East and Central Asia. Pistachio-rich desserts such as baklava, Turkish delight and kulfi are testament to the nut's heritage.

Ideas for using pistachios:
- Blend with parmesan to make a crust for meats.
- Use in pesto instead of pine nuts.
- Relax by shelling a bowl of salted pistachios with a beer at the end of a summer's day.

9. PUMPKIN SEEDS

Otherwise known as pepitas, pumpkin seeds are at their best when pumpkins are in season. They are an excellent source of vitamin E and a good source of minerals such as iron, magnesium and manganese.

Ideas for using pumpkin seeds:
- Candy them or use in praline.
- Sprinkle over salads.
- Sprinkle on top of muffins or bread before baking.

10. SESAME SEEDS

Sesame seeds have a strong nutty and earthy flavour, and are available in black and white varieties. They're also a great source of calcium.

Ideas for using sesame seeds:
- Sprinkle over stir-fries or Asian salads.
- Toast them and sprinkle on roasted vegetables.
- Make sesame and flaxseed crackers (see page 74).

11. SUNFLOWER SEEDS

Sunflower seeds are the best wholefood source of vitamin E.

Ideas for using sunflower seeds:
- Sprinkle over salads.
- Grind into a nut butter (see page 68).

12. WALNUTS

Incredibly nutrient dense, a quarter of a cup of walnuts contains 90 per cent of the recommended daily intake of omega-3 fats.

Ideas for using walnuts:
- Roast and combine with figs and soft cheese in a salad.
- Sprinkle over porridge with raisins.

BUCKWHEAT AND BARLEY LOAF – THANKS AGAIN PAULY!

Pauly, our original bread supplier from Bronte, and now close friend, is once again supplying us with sourdough and epic croissants at our new restaurant at The Farm in Byron Bay. Teaming up with his mates Sammy and Tom, The Bread Social brings us delicious baked goodness every morning. This beautiful, low-gluten loaf has been a real standout – it's wholesome, nutrient-rich and packed with flavour. You can halve this recipe if you like, however the bread freezes exceptionally well. All of the measurements here, even the water, are in grams – this is because it's really important to be as precise as possible. You will need to start this recipe the day before.

Grain soak
80 g pearl barley
80 g buckwheat
40 g sorghum
25 g honey
180 g lukewarm water

Pre-ferment
100 g baker's flour
2 g dried yeast
100 g cold water

Buckwheat bread dough
390 g buckwheat flour
390 g baker's flour
20 g salt
485 g lukewarm water
200 g pre-ferment
  (or sourdough starter)
400 g grain soak

For the grain soak, combine the barley, buckwheat and sorghum in a container large enough for the grains to expand by half again. Dissolve the honey in the water and pour over the top of the grains. Cover loosely and stand overnight at room temperature.

If you have your own sourdough starter, then by all means use it in this recipe. If you don't, a simple pre-ferment will give the dough all the activity you need, as well as adding a little acidity. Mix the flour and yeast in a bowl large enough for the mix to triple in size. Add the water and combine until even, making sure that all the flour is hydrated. Cover loosely and refrigerate overnight.

When you check on the progress the next day, the grains will have absorbed all the liquid, and the pre-ferment should be very active and have a slightly sour smell.

To make the bread dough, add the buckwheat flour, baker's flour and salt to a large bowl and combine. Add the water and 200 g of the pre-ferment. Fold the components together, working until the dough is a consistent mass – buckwheat flour has no gluten, so you won't get the elastic dough that you would using only baker's flour. Knead the dough for about 5 minutes in the bowl. It should now be a fairly smooth piece of dough. Tip 400 g of the soaked grains over the dough and incorporate them by repeatedly folding the dough over itself. Once all the grains are evenly distributed, remove the dough, and lightly grease the bowl with a neutral or mild oil. Place the dough back in the bowl and cover. Set aside for 2 hours for the dough to rest and prove.

Oil or line two 13.5-cm × 10-cm (11-cm deep) bread tins.

After 2 hours, portion out two 940 g pieces of dough. On a lightly floured work surface, elongate each piece into rectangles running lengthways away from the edge of the bench. Roll the top of each piece of dough towards you – try to make the roll as tight as you can without tearing the dough. Where the roll finishes is known as the seam. Place each loaf, seam-side down, into the bread tins. Cover and set aside for 2 hours.

Preheat the oven to 170°C fan-forced (190°C conventional). Place a baking tray on the bottom shelf of the oven.

Once the dough has risen to around 2 cm below the lip of each tin, place the tins in the oven. Pour 2 cups of water into the hot baking tray and close the door. The steam generated will help the loaf expand, as well as dissolve the sugars on the surface of the dough and allow them to caramelise, resulting in a darker, more flavoursome crust. The loaves will take approximately 1 hour to bake. If your oven has hotspots, the loaves may require rotating.

Remove from the oven and rest for 5 minutes before tipping out of the tins onto a cooling rack. The loaves should stand for at least 4 hours before slicing to allow the crumb to set. The bread will last for 1 week in a sealed bag at room temperature or up to 2 months tightly wrapped in the freezer.

Makes 2 × 940 g loaves

How to make
NUT BUTTER

Nut butters are a great way to add the benefits of nuts to your diet in a simple spread. You can turn absolutely any nut, raw or roasted, into butter. All you'll need is a high-power blender and a little grapeseed or melted coconut oil to help the butter blend properly. I also like to add a good pinch of salt to really bring out the flavour, but it's up to you. I suggest using 400 g of nuts at a minimum so that the blender has something to work with. How much oil you'll need really depends on the nuts and how much natural oil they have. With peanuts, for example, I usually don't have to add any oil at all. You'll see pretty quickly if it needs it or not. We can't make nut butter quickly enough in my house, but it's best to make it in smaller batches to keep the oils fresh. Spread it on toast and crackers, or smear it on a banana and drizzle over some honey. It's also great with grains or to dip fresh cut vegies in, and homemade peanut butter makes amazing satay sauce.

You'll need:
  400 g your choice of nuts, roasted and cooled (or raw, if you prefer, but we like the
  extra flavour that roasting adds)
  salt flakes
  grapeseed or coconut oil, as needed

Makes 400 g

Add the nuts and a pinch of salt to a blender and process for about 2 minutes.

The nuts will be quite fine by now, and will have heated up slightly and released their oil.

As the nuts form a paste, add a little oil if it needs loosening.

Keep blending, adjusting with more coconut oil if needed, until you have the desired consistency. Season to taste.

Spoon into a jar to cool. Enjoy on crusty sourdough bread!

You can use almost any kind of nut to make nut butter – almonds, pistachios, hazelnuts and brazil nuts all work really well.

GO NUTS MAKING YOUR OWN NUT BUTTER!

RUSTIC CRISPBREAD

These store well without needing any artificial preservatives, their non-uniform shape gives them a nicely rustic feel, and they taste incredible. They also go really well with cheese. Keep the base recipe the same but try playing with different combinations instead of sesame seeds: they're delicious sprinkled with dukkah; with rosemary and thyme; or you can use a mix of nuts and seeds. It helps to use a pasta machine to make these, as rolling dough out to 1-mm thick can be somewhat of a skill in itself. The measurements here may seem quite precise, but it's always best to be particular with a recipe like this, right down to weighing the water.

500 g plain flour
40 g extra virgin olive oil
15 g salt flakes, plus extra for sprinkling
10 g baker's yeast
10 g black and white sesame seeds, plus extra for sprinkling
240 g warm water

Combine all the ingredients in the bowl of an electric mixer. Mix with the dough hook for 15 minutes until smooth. Wrap the dough in plastic wrap and rest in the fridge for 1–2 hours.

Preheat the oven to 180°C fan-forced (200°C conventional). Line two baking trays with baking paper.

Unwrap the dough and portion it into 75 g pieces. Using a pasta machine or rolling pin, roll out each piece of dough until 1–2-mm thick and place on the prepared trays. Sprinkle generously with salt and sesame seeds and bake for 12 minutes or until slightly golden and very crisp.

Makes about 10 large crispbreads

SESAME AND FLAXSEED CRACKERS

This recipe is something I learnt years ago, and I've been using it consistently ever since. It's dead easy, and will make you look like a pro when you use them on your next cheese plate. They're also pretty cool for a snack and unreal in kid's lunch boxes. The measurements here may seem quite precise, but it's always best to be particular with a recipe like this, right down to weighing the water.

280 g wholemeal flour
140 g rolled oats
100 g flaxseeds
100 g sesame seeds
20 g sunflower seeds
5 g za'atar*
5 g dried rosemary
10 g salt
345 g warm water

* Za'atar is a Middle Eastern spice mix that contains thyme, oregano, sumac, sesame seeds and other spices. It's available from Middle Eastern grocers and some supermarkets.

Add the dry ingredients to the bowl of a stand mixer and mix with the dough hook for 2 minutes. Add the water and mix for another 5–6 minutes until smooth and well combined. Wrap the dough in plastic wrap and rest for a good 10 minutes on the bench.

Preheat the oven to 170°C fan-forced – this recipe really needs the even heat from fan-forced cooking, otherwise the crackers won't dry out properly. Line two baking trays with baking paper.

Once rested, cut the dough in half to make it easier to work. Using a pasta machine or rolling pin, roll out each piece until about 3-mm thick. Dock the dough by pricking it randomly with the tines of a fork – this stops it bubbling up while baking – and cut into desired shapes, being aware that the crackers will shrink a little. Bake for about 12 minutes until pale golden and cooked all the way through. If you've rolled the dough a little thicker, they'll just need to bake a little longer. Rest until cool and crisp.

Store in an airtight container until required. These will last close to a year if you've cooked and stored them correctly.

Makes about 300 g

BIRDSEED BARS

My Nan used to have a bird table on her front lawn. As a treat, she would pour the fat from the Sunday roast into a cup with piece of string poking out of it and set it in the fridge. When it was set, she would gently warm the cup and empty the solid block of fat onto a wooden board. Next she would roll the whole thing in chopped nuts and seeds and tie the winter treat to the bird table. As a kid I thought that was truly amazing, though not as much as the birds did.

These bars are really handy to have around before early morning surfs, or just as a snack on the run. It may look like a lot of ingredients, but it's a recipe that can be played around with. So long as you keep the wet and dry ratios the same, you'll get the right consistency. Feel free to use raisins or dried figs instead of cranberries and dates. Or swap the seeds around with chia, sesame or poppy seeds.

100 g rolled oats
60 g raw almonds
4 tablespoons shredded coconut
3 tablespoons pumpkin seeds
3 teaspoons flaxseeds
3 tablespoons sunflower seeds
60 g honey
60 g peanut butter
50 g dried cranberries
50 g pitted dates
1 pinch of salt flakes

Preheat the oven to 200°C fan-forced (220°C conventional). Grease a 25-cm loaf tin and line with baking paper.

Spread the oats and almonds out on a baking tray and roast for 10 minutes. Spread the coconut, pumpkin seeds, flaxseeds and sunflower seeds on another tray and roast for 3 minutes. Combine the roasted oats, nuts and seeds in a large bowl.

Add the honey, peanut butter, cranberries, dates and salt to a blender and blend to a paste. Add 3 tablespoons of the roasted mix and blend until smooth.

Add the pureed mix to the dry mix and combine with your hands. Transfer to the prepared tin, place some paper on top and press down firmly to compact. Chill for at least 3 hours before turning out and slicing into bars. These will keep well in the fridge for a couple of weeks.

Makes 10 bars

CRUNCHY NUT SNAPS

This is a great way of incorporating a lot of nuts and seeds into your diet without any of the refined sugar or preservatives that you find in commercial nut bars. They stay crunchy for a few weeks stored in an airtight container and are great as an office snack, or for the school lunchbox.

110 g Brazil nuts
110 g cashews, unsalted
110 g raw almonds
110 g hazelnuts
2 eggwhites
100 g raw honey
90 g shredded coconut
2 tablespoons flaxseeds
3 tablespoons sesame seeds
30 g (1 cup) puffed rice

Preheat the oven to 180°C fan-forced (200°C conventional). Line a large baking tray with baking paper.

Spread the nuts out on the lined tray and roast for about 15 minutes, checking and tossing every 5 minutes. Set aside to cool completely.

Reduce the oven temperature to 100°C fan-forced (120°C conventional). Line a baking tray with baking paper.

Whip the eggwhites until stiff peaks form. Gradually add the honey and stir gently until you have a velvety mix.

In a blender or food processor, pulse the cooled nuts until lightly crushed but not pulverized.

Combine the coconut, flaxseeds, sesame seeds, puffed rice and crushed nuts in a large bowl and fold in the whipped eggwhite mix. Spread the mixture over the prepared tray, pressing it into the base and corners to make an even 1.5-cm thick sheet. Bake for 2½ hours.

Remove from the oven and cool completely. Break into long pieces and store in an airtight glass jar.

Makes 700 g

CACAO AND COCONUT SUPER-BALLS

I first started making these when I was part of Frank's cycling squad in the eastern suburbs of Sydney. I still chuckle when I think about these chicken legs wrapped in Lycra at 5:30 am, but I loved it. Those early morning squad sessions were an interesting contrast between the gentle, misty beauty of the awakening city and fifty grown men in Lycra grunting and barging into each other for position. After a particularly gruelling training session, I was handed a commercially made protein snack, and I was horrified at the taste of it. I started making my own natural protein snacks to pick me up when Franky was in an exceptionally bad mood. This is one of my favourites.

100 g dates, pitted
100 g prunes, pitted
100 g coconut oil
200 g desiccated coconut
50 g chia seeds
50 g cacao powder
3½ tablespoons cacao nibs
1 tablespoon honey
1 tablespoon maca powder
1 tablespoon bee pollen

Add the dates, prunes and coconut oil to a blender and process until a smooth paste forms.

Add the date paste to a large bowl with half the desiccated coconut and the remaining ingredients. Using your hands, mix until combined and then roll into walnut-sized balls. Roll the balls in the remaining desiccated coconut and refrigerate to firm up. These will keep for a couple of months in the fridge.

Makes 20 balls

CURRY

& SPICE

A GUIDE TO OUR FAVOURITE

Spices

MARK: My Sri Lankan Grandmother, Nana Barney, used to make a curry that was so spicy it made your eyeballs ache and your hands clammy. My brother Grant and I grew up watching her cook curries. She would buy big mud crabs from the fish market and let them loose in her backyard while she prepared the spices. We'd chase those crabs around the banana palm and curry trees, and when we looked towards the house we could see Nana Barney through the window, grinding cardamom pods and frying coriander seeds. She would leave the door open, and the smells from the house made us hungry. Finally she'd call us in, and we'd bring the crabs and watch her break them down and throw them into the pot.

The food we cook is a culmination of the places we've been and the people we've met. We are constantly tying to recreate these food memories, and so many of them are triggered by the mouthwatering smell of certain spices. It's remarkable to think that these dried fragments of tropical plants have been the motivation for wars, exploration and trade since the beginning of civilisation. Hunted across continents, spices were sent back to royal courts as exotic trophies from mysterious lands. They were traded on spice routes and used for medicine, perfume, incense and flavouring. So revered were they during the Middle Ages that any spice merchant caught cutting his saffron with safflower, thistle seed or turmeric was burned at the stake.

The spice narrative has long since departed from its ancient purity. An increase in demand and a desire for convenience has led to the adulteration of spices into products that are highly processed and diluted. Most people now know spices as those faintly scented powders consigned to the back of their cupboards. If you breathe deeply enough, they hint at a more vibrant life before they were processed into bottles and stored on supermarket shelves. The truth is, grocery store turnover of spices isn't fast enough to ensure their freshness, so where possible, buy whole spices and grind them as you need them. Use a mortar and pestle or a cheap coffee grinder. If you don't have a local spice merchant, go to ethnic markets or buy them online. To retain freshness, store spices in good quality sealed containers, in a cool, dark place. Choose glass containers where possible, as plastic can be too porous. This is particularly important for ground spices, where the process of grinding immediately starts the release of flavour. Avoid using a wet spoon when scooping spices out, as this can cause them to become lumpy or mouldy.

Aside from the gastronomical potential of spices, there are other reasons to use them: they make healthy food more appealing; they reduce the need for salt without sacrificing taste; and spices like chilli and ginger enhance metabolism. So, how do you activate spices? You grind them, pound them, grate them, infuse them or dry roast them. Doing this ruptures the cell walls and releases their essential oils. A classic example is the humble curry. When you fry whole cardamom pods, coriander seeds and cinnamon bark, the heat activates so much flavour that the kitchen comes alive.

Cooking with spices can seem intimidating. What goes with what? How much of each? And what on earth is fenugreek? The best advice we can give is to learn to understand the different characteristics of individual spices. See over the page for flavour profiles of some of our favourite spices. Mixing spices will require some kitchen play to work out if you want to add a bit more of this or a little less of that. We treat spices as key ingredients, layering them into dishes and then tasting to make sure we haven't got too carried away. See page 92 for some basic recipes for spice mixes to start playing with.

1. BAY

Originally from the Mediterranean, the bay leaf is pungently aromatic and can seem both bitter and sweet. It is used whole, chopped or ground to a powder. Bay is slow to release its flavour, so it works well in slow-cooked dishes, like broths, soups, braises and curries. It can also add interesting spice to sweet recipes, like fruit compotes and jams. Bay leaves are leathery and tough to chew, so if you're using them whole, remove from the dish before eating.

2. CARDAMOM

A member of the ginger family, green or true cardamom has an intensely sweet flavour. Cardamom is used as a whole pod or the seeds are ground to a powder. It is great in curries and rice dishes, but equally as good in desserts and hot drinks, such as chai. Cardamom pairs well with cinnamon, ginger, turmeric and cumin.

3. CINNAMON

Cinnamon is the dried bark of various kinds of laurel tree, such as cassia. While true cinnamon is native to Sri Lanka, different types of cassia cinnamon are grown across Asia and Central America. It is used in cooking as a dried bark or powder. Cinnamon is sweet and bitter and works really well in cakes, pastries and desserts, but also in savoury preparations, such as curries and pickles. Cinnamon pairs well with ginger, nutmeg, cloves and allspice.

4. CUMIN

A member of the parsley family, cumin has a hot, earthy and bitter taste. Cumin works really well in spicy food, such as Mexican dishes, and pairs well with chilli powder, cinnamon, ginger, coriander, turmeric and garlic.

5. FENUGREEK

Best used alongside other spices, fenugreek has a bitter, almost maple syrup-like flavour. It works well in tomato-based sauces, dry rubs and breads, and it pairs well with coriander, paprika and cumin. Fenugreek is often sold as 'methi' in Asian and Middle Eastern grocers.

6. GROUND GINGER

Ground ginger is created when the peeled fresh ginger root is dried and ground to a power. Ground ginger is hot, sweet and bitter and has incredible anti-inflammatory properties. It is used in tagines, spice rubs and sauces, as well as in myriad desserts, teas and drinks.

7. MUSTARD

There are three types of mustard, all with yellow flowers and small seeds: yellow, brown and black. Yellow mustard is mellower, brown mustard is more pungent, and black is the most strongly flavoured. Mustard pairs well with bay, cumin, fenugreek, garlic and turmeric.

8. NUTMEG

From the brown seed of the nutmeg tree, nutmeg is most commonly used in cooking as a ground powder. It is similar in taste to cinnamon but with a stronger, more 'bitey' profile. It pairs really well with cinnamon, ginger and vanilla in cakes and desserts, however it also goes well with coriander, cumin and cardamom in stews and soups.

9. PAPRIKA

From a mild red chilli in the capsicum family, paprika is available in varieties ranging from sweet and mild, to pungent and spicy. It goes well with meat, and is often used to season and colour soups and rice dishes. It pairs well with chilli powder, cumin, cardamom, garlic and cinnamon.

10. SUMAC

Sumac is made from the red berries of the sumac bush, native to the Middle East, which are dried and ground to a powder. With a tangy citrus flavour, sumac works well with meats, in dry rubs and in spice mixes, like za'atar. Sprinkle it over vegetables or Middle Eastern dips, like hummus.

11. TURMERIC

Typically used in its dried and powdered form, turmeric contains strong medicinal properties and is sometimes referred to as poor man's saffron for its power to colour food a rich, custardy yellow. It has an aromatic, bitter taste and is an essential ingredient in many Asian curries. Turmeric pairs well with chilli powder, garlic, ginger, nutmeg, paprika, allspice, coriander and cumin.

ROASTED CAULIFLOWER WITH CHILLI AND MUSTARD SEEDS

A good Indian curry night is all about the little side dishes: saag aloo, pappadums, mango chutney, cucumber raita and, of course, spiced cauliflower, which is one of my favourite sides. I could easily eat it as a snack on its own. It's important to crank the oven up so it's nice and hot. Ideally, with the cauliflower coated in all the spices and butter, it'll char up a little in the oven. You could also do this on the barbecue with the lid closed.

I small cauliflower, cut into small florets
I tablespoon vegetable oil
2 garlic cloves, finely sliced
I teaspoon yellow mustard seeds
I long green chilli, finely sliced
½ teaspoon ground cumin
½ teaspoon ground turmeric
I tablespoon butter
salt flakes and freshly ground pepper
I spring onion, finely sliced on an angle
I tablespoon roughly chopped almonds
I tablespoon chopped coriander leaves
½ lime

Preheat the oven to 200°C fan-forced (220°C conventional).

Cook the cauliflower in boiling salted water for 2 minutes. Remove from the water with a strainer or slotted spoon, so that the florets hold their shape, and set aside to cool in a colander. Don't refresh with cold water, as you want the cauliflower to dry out and retain its flavour.

Heat the oil in a non-stick frying pan over medium–low heat and gently fry the garlic for 1–2 minutes. Just as it turns slightly golden, add the mustard seeds. Once they've popped, remove from the heat and add the chilli, cumin, turmeric and butter to the pan and stir to combine.

Add the cauliflower to a large bowl and pour the spiced oil and butter mix over the top. Season and gently toss to ensure the cauliflower is well coated. Spread out on a baking tray and roast for 10–15 minutes or until slightly charred and tender.

Transfer the cauliflower to a serving platter and top with the spring onion, almonds and coriander. Squeeze over the lime and serve.

Serves 4–6 as a side

EGG HOPPERS

My Nan used to make egg hoppers for my brother and me when we stayed with her. She used to buy them from the street corner in Colombo, but after migrating to Australia it wasn't that simple, so she learnt how to make them, and she was the guru. To this day, her hoppers are still the best I've ever eaten (and I've eaten plenty of them from the street corners of Colombo as well). Hoppers are amazing filled with pretty much any curry and coconut sambal. They're similar to a taco in that you fold them over and eat the whole thing. The trick is not to load them up too much. Definitely no knives and forks for this one.

25 g fresh yeast (or if you can only get dried, use 2 × 7 g sachets)
1 good pinch of sugar
400 ml coconut milk
500 g rice flour
1 pinch of salt
1 handful of desiccated coconut
5 eggwhites
vegetable oil, to fry
12–16 eggs

Coconut sambal
50 g desiccated coconut
1 teaspoon chilli powder
½ handful of coriander leaves, chopped
½ red onion, finely sliced
juice of ½ lemon

For this recipe, you will need a hopper pan (small bowl-shaped pan with a lid), which are available from any good Indian or Sri Lankan food store for about $5.

Mix the yeast and sugar with 100 ml of warm water in a large bowl and stir until smooth. Add the coconut milk and set aside for about 30 minutes.

Add the rice flour, salt and 100 ml of warm water and set aside for a minimum of 2–3 hours in a warm place. The mix will froth up and almost double in size.

To make the coconut sambal, mix all the ingredients in a small bowl.

When you're ready to make the hoppers, mix in the desiccated coconut. Whip the eggwhites until just at soft peaks and fold into the mix.

Place the hopper pan over high heat. Lightly rub the inside of the pan with a cloth dipped in vegetable oil, making sure that it doesn't pool in the bottom of the pan. Add a ladle of the hopper batter (about 60 ml) and swirl to cover the whole pan – it will start to bubble slightly and be able to support its own weight up the sides of the pan as it cooks. Gently crack an egg in the centre of the pan and put the lid on. Reduce the heat so the flame has the same circumference as the egg – this will centralise the heat to focus on cooking the egg without burning the batter. Check the egg after a minute or so, the white of the egg should be well on its way to being cooked, monitor it, making sure not to cook the yolk. Remove from the pan and repeat.

The beauty of this is you can make a few at a time and serve them at room temperature; when the hot curry goes in it will warm everything up again. To serve, spoon in your choice of curry, the coconut sambal and some grilled cucumber and mint yoghurt (see page 190).

Serves 6

CHICKEN, PUMPKIN AND CASHEW CURRY

This recipe comes from a very good friend of mine, Lynette Macdonald, who I met years ago at a Tetsuya's Christmas party. She's one of the most passionate food people I have ever met. Lynette has a tiny kitchen, but always has a dozen or so food projects on the go. She sold me my first Thermomix, and has shared many recipes, tips and crazy food ideas over the years. This is one of the best chicken curries I've tasted. It may seem like a large amount of curry powder but trust me, it works!

3 tablespoons ghee
  (or vegetable oil)
1 large onion, finely sliced
4 garlic cloves
5-cm piece of ginger
10–15 curry leaves (optional)
3 kaffir lime leaves
1 bunch of coriander, leaves
  picked and roots and stalks
  reserved
1 lemongrass stem, white part
  only
1 × 1.6 kg chicken, cut into
  10–12 pieces, skin on and
  bones in
200 ml coconut milk (or
  coconut cream)
500 g peeled and deseeded
  pumpkin, cut into 5-cm dice
400 g can diced tomatoes
100 g roasted cashews
1 heaped teaspoon salt flakes

Curry powder
75 g coriander seeds
50 g cumin seeds
8 green cardamom pods
1 cinnamon stick
4 cloves
6 black peppercorns
½ teaspoon ground turmeric
1–2 dried chillies
½ teaspoon Kashmiri chilli
  powder* (optional)

* *Kashmiri chillies are generally
  used to add a lovely red colour to
  a dish; they are quite mild and are
  available from Indian spice shops.
  A tablespoon of tomato paste can
  be used instead — just add it to
  the saucepan at the same time as
  the curry powder.*

For the curry powder, toast the coriander seeds, cumin seeds, cardamom, cinnamon and cloves in a dry frying pan until fragrant and lightly coloured.

Tip the spices into a blender or spice grinder with the remaining curry powder ingredients and process to a fine powder.

Place a large saucepan over medium heat, add the ghee and fry the onion until it's just turning golden. Add the curry powder and cook over medium heat for about 8 minutes, stirring frequently to ensure the spices don't burn.

Meanwhile, place the garlic, ginger, curry leaves, lime leaves, coriander roots and stalks, and lemongrass in a blender and blitz to a paste.

Add the paste to the pan and fry for a few minutes until fragrant. Add the chicken, coconut milk, pumpkin, tomatoes, cashews, salt and half the coriander leaves. Slowly simmer over low heat for 45 minutes, stirring occasionally.

Sprinkle with the remaining coriander leaves and serve with steamed rice.

Serves 4–6

SPICE MIXES

Here are some of our favourite spice mixes to get you started. The more you play around with these, the more confident you'll get and the more brazen and adventurous you will become.

Basic curry spice mix

2 tablespoons ground coriander
2 tablespoons ground cumin
2 teaspoons ground turmeric
1 teaspoon salt
½ teaspoon chilli powder
½ teaspoon ground cardamom
½ teaspoon ground ginger
½ teaspoon mustard seeds

Simply mix all the ingredients in a small bowl. Store in a glass jar and use in any number of ways: sprinkle over flatbreads before cooking; use to coat veggies before roasting or chargrilling; add to vinaigrettes and salad dressings; or add a pinch to the rice cooker when cooking rice for extra flavour.

Dukkah rub for fish or chicken

100 g coriander seeds
100 g cumin seeds
100 g sesame seeds
50 g fennel seeds
3 tablespoons finely chopped roasted hazelnuts
ground white pepper

Toast the seeds in a dry frying pan until fragrant and lightly coloured. Grind roughly using a mortar and pestle. Add the hazelnuts and ground white pepper to taste. Sprinkle generously over fish or chicken before cooking.

Coffee rub for meat

1 tablespoon cumin seeds
1 tablespoon coriander seeds
1 tablespoon smoked paprika
1 tablespoon garlic powder
1 pinch of chilli powder
1 tablespoon salt flakes
1 tablespoon brown sugar
1 tablespoon ground coffee

Toast the cumin and coriander seeds in a dry frying pan until fragrant and lightly coloured. Tip into a mortar and grind to a powder. Add the remaining ingredients and combine. See page 136 for slow-cooked brisket using this rub.

INDIAN BEEF SHORT RIB CURRY

We all like a one-pot wonder, no fuss and minimal washing up. This one's a real wintery dish, great for those cold nights. Come home from work, fifteen minutes to prep, pop it in the oven and forget about it while you kick back, crack open a bottle of wine and unwind for a few hours … yep, if only life was so simple. So, once you've finished chasing the dog or kids or partner around the house, done the washing, cleaning, paid the bills and read the emails, and your curry is almost ready, add a tin of drained chickpeas to warm through, add a little yoghurt and coriander, sit down and enjoy. If you can't find ribs, try beef cheeks, oxtail or crosscut veal shanks.

1 tablespoon vegetable oil
salt flakes and freshly
   ground pepper
1.5 kg beef short ribs
   (or 8 short ribs)
2 onions, finely chopped
6 garlic cloves, finely sliced
1 teaspoon ground turmeric
1 tablespoon ground
   coriander
1 tablespoon ground cumin
2 star anise
½ teaspoon chilli powder
1 cinnamon stick
5-cm piece of ginger, finely
   grated
400 g can diced tomatoes
1 tablespoon honey
500 ml chicken stock
400 g can chickpeas, drained
100 g natural yoghurt
½ bunch of coriander, leaves
   picked and torn

Preheat the oven to 180°C fan-forced (200°C conventional).

Heat the oil in a heavy-based, ovenproof pan over medium–high heat. Season the ribs and brown on all sides. Remove the ribs and reduce the heat to medium. Add the onion and garlic and cook for 4–5 minutes. Add the spices and ginger and cook for a couple of minutes while stirring. Return the ribs to the dish and add the tomatoes, honey, stock and 400 ml of water. Cover with foil or a lid and place in the oven for 2–3 hours – the ribs are ready when the meat is tender and comes away from the bone.

Remove the ribs from the dish and adjust the consistency by reducing the liquid on the stovetop. Once reduced, add the chickpeas to the curry and warm through. Add the ribs back to the dish and stir through half the yoghurt and coriander.

Serve the curry with the remaining yoghurt and coriander, and jasmine or brown rice on the side.

Serves 4

CHICKEN CURRY IN A HURRY

Coming from the UK, I'm obsessed with curry. As a kid, if my Mum was cooking curry we would get really excited. I remember her joining a curry club and being really passionate about experimenting with different recipes. Well, there are thousands of curry recipes out there, from all over the world. This one is a good one to start with, nothing too tricky, with readily available ingredients.

1 teaspoon fennel seeds
2 teaspoons cumin seeds
2 teaspoons coriander seeds
1 teaspoons ground turmeric
1 teaspoon garam masala
12 curry leaves
3 tablespoons ghee (or vegetable oil), plus extra
2 onions, roughly chopped
5 garlic cloves
60 g ginger
1 long red chilli, stalk removed
1 bunch of coriander, leaves picked and stalks reserved
4 green cardamom pods
400 g can diced tomatoes
300 ml chicken stock
800 g chicken thigh fillets, cut into bite-sized dice
fish sauce, to season
soy sauce, to season
200 g natural yoghurt
1 tablespoon toasted flaked almonds (optional)
1 lime

Toast the fennel, cumin and coriander seeds in a dry frying pan until fragrant and lightly coloured.

Using a spice grinder or mortar and pestle, grind the spices to a powder. Mix in the turmeric and garam masala.

Fry the curry leaves in a little ghee until fragrant.

Add the curry leaves to a blender with the onion, garlic, ginger, chilli, coriander stalks and 3 tablespoons of ghee. Blend to a smooth paste.

In a large saucepan, gently fry the garlic and ginger paste, cardamom and ground spices for 6–8 minutes, stirring constantly with a wooden spoon to prevent it catching. Add the tomatoes and cook for 5 minutes. Pour in the chicken stock and cook until slightly thickened, about 10 minutes. When you're happy with the thickness of the sauce, add the chicken, turn the heat down to low and simmer for 8–10 minutes.

Once the chicken is cooked, season to taste with fish sauce and soy sauce. Stir through half the yoghurt and half the coriander leaves.

To serve, sprinkle over the almonds (if using) and remaining coriander, squeeze over the lime, drizzle with the remaining yoghurt and serve with steamed basmati rice.

Serves 4

FISH
& SEAFOOD

SALT AND PEPPER SQUID WITH BLACK GARLIC AIOLI

This dish should be on everybody's hit list. It's easy, it's delicious, it's impressive to people who have never made it before, and it's a great intro to seafood for the little ones when they say they don't like it. The black garlic brings another element to the aioli with its unique sweetly aromatic characteristics, while the squid ink darkens the complexion and adds depth.

4 large squid, cleaned, tentacles kept

1.5 litres frying oil (canola or cottonseed, you can even use coconut)

350 g plain flour

55 g salt flakes

1½ tablespoons ground black pepper

1 teaspoon sweet paprika

1 teaspoon chilli powder (optional)

2 long red chillies, deseeded and julienned

½ bunch of coriander, leaves picked

¼ bunch of spring onions, green part only, finely sliced on an angle

2 lemons, halved

Black garlic aioli

2 egg yolks

2 teaspoons Dijon mustard

2 tablespoons white vinegar

250 ml grapeseed oil

½ black garlic bulb, base sliced off and cloves squeezed out

½ teaspoon squid ink (optional)

juice of ½ lemon (optional)

salt flakes and freshly ground pepper

To make the aioli, add the yolks, mustard and vinegar to a food processor and process for 2 minutes. Slowly start adding the oil while processing, as it emulsifies the mix will thicken considerably. After you've added two-thirds of the oil, add the garlic and squid ink (if using) while processing. If the aioli is runny, keep adding oil; if it's too thick, add a little lemon juice. Season to taste.

Using a sharp knife, score the squid tubes in a crisscross pattern partially into the flesh (this will help it curl up when fried) and cut into bite-sized pieces – just skip the scoring step if you don't feel confident with your knife skills. Separate the tentacles and cut into manageable lengths.

Heat the oil in a large wok or saucepan over high heat until 180–190°C.

Mix the flour, salt, pepper, paprika and chilli powder (if using) in a large bowl. Toss the squid in the flour mix, giving it a good coating. Dust off lightly and carefully lower into the hot oil – do this in small (perhaps three) batches, as the oil temperature will drop if you try to cook it all at once. Cook for 2–3 minutes, depending on the size of the squid, being careful not to cook it for too long, as it will become rubbery. Drain on paper towel.

Plate the squid, scatter over the fresh chilli, coriander and spring onion, and serve with the aioli and lemon wedges on the side.

Any leftover aioli will keep in the fridge for 4–5 days. Use it in chicken sandwiches, drizzled over a tray of roasted vegetable with fresh herbs or, of course, for more salt and pepper squid.

Serves 4

CRAYFISH BISQUE

This is a lovely dish to make when you have a few crayfish heads lying around in the freezer. After a good winter season diving for crayfish, we only eat the tails in our house, but as the crays become scarce, we start to make a few more bisques to try and extend the season. Even though I've taken my girlfriend Hannah diving a few times, she always used to say that she'd never seen a crayfish, not even a small one. And it wasn't until I made this dish for her the first time that she realised that they're green before they're cooked. She'd been looking for red crays the whole time. I thought that was pretty funny, to be honest.

5 crayfish heads, and tail shells
   if you have them
60 ml vegetable oil
1 large onion, roughly chopped
6 garlic cloves, roughly
   chopped
3 long red chillies, roughly
   chopped
2 tablespoons tomato paste
1 teaspoon sweet paprika
250 g cherry tomatoes
2 litres chicken stock
90 ml dry sherry
300 ml cream
freshly chopped chives,
   to serve

Preheat the oven to 200°C fan-forced (220°C conventional).

Roughly chop the heads and shells. Add to a roasting tray and roast for at least 20 minutes until the shells turn a deep red and the mustard in the heads caramelises — watch this fairly carefully, as you want an intensely roasted flavour but no burnt character.

Add the oil to a large saucepan over medium–high heat. Add the onion, garlic and chilli and cook until softened. Add the tomato paste and paprika and stir constantly, making sure it doesn't stick. Add the roasted cray shells and tomatoes to the pan and, as you stir, smash up the heads with your spoon.

Place the roasting tray over a burner and deglaze with some of the chicken stock.

Add the sherry to the pan and reduce for 30 seconds. Add the deglazed liquid from the tray, along with the remaining stock and simmer for 1–2 hours — this may seem like a big variable in timing, but you'll get a good result after an hour, and if you carefully watch the bisque and add a little water as needed, another hour will really deepen the flavour.

Strain the stock through a fine sieve into a clean saucepan. You should have around 1 litre, maybe a bit more, and it should have thickened considerably. Season well and stir in the cream. Reheat and serve with a sprinkling of chives.

For a more complete meal, poach your favourite fish in the stock before adding the cream. Place a handful of cooked wild rice or mixed grains into serving bowls, add the poached fish and pour the bisque over the top.

Makes about 1.5 litres

LEATHERJACKET BRANDADE

Brandade is a hearty emulsion of fish (traditionally salt cod) and olive oil, thickened with potatoes or bread. For our recipe, we wanted to use a fish that barely gets a look-in on restaurant menus: good old leatherjacket. It's a plentiful and under-utilised fish that's almost always at the market, and it's incredibly cheap. At Tetsuya's, we used to marinate leatherjacket in a little ginger, garlic, soy and mirin, and then fry the fillets. But I've also found that with a little care you can also prepare a stunning brandade. Serve with toasted sourdough, pickles and a bitter leaf salad.

400 g leatherjacket fillets
   (or any white-fleshed fish),
   skin removed
salt flakes
1 garlic clove, peeled and
   bruised
¼ teaspoon black peppercorns
1 fresh bay leaf
3 lemon verbena leaves
   (optional)
300 ml milk
60 g sourdough bread,
   crusts removed
finely grated zest and juice
   of 1 lemon
80 ml olive oil
1 tablespoon chopped
   flat-leaf parsley
1 pinch of cayenne pepper
ground white pepper

Season the fish and add to a medium saucepan with the garlic, peppercorns, bay leaf, lemon verbena (if using) and milk over low heat. Once the milk is just gently ticking over, poach the fish for 4–6 minutes – don't let the milk boil. Turn off the heat and set aside for 2–3 minutes.

Lift the fish out of the milk and flake the meat into a food processor, being careful to remove any bones. Strain the milk into a medium bowl and add the bread. Set aside to soak for a few minutes.

Strain the bread (reserving a little of the milk), but don't squeeze the milk out, and add to the food processor with the fish. Add the lemon zest, and blend while adding the olive oil and lemon juice until a spreadable consistency. If you need to loosen the brandade a little, just add a little of the reserved poaching milk. Add the parsley and season with cayenne pepper, salt and white pepper.

Serve on toasted sourdough with pickles or spoon into a glass jar and refrigerate.

Makes 2.5 cups

BRAISED AND CHARRED OCTOPUS

This is a dish that needs a bit of time in advance to get organised, but it's well worth it in the end. I like to serve this with boiled herbed potatoes and a few bitter greens, but the combinations are endless: with a salad, risotto or just on its own.

1 tablespoon vegetable oil
2 red onions, finely sliced
1 tablespoon minced garlic
1 long red chilli, finely sliced
salt flakes and freshly
　　ground pepper
olive oil, for grilling
1 large handful of flat-leaf
　　parsley, leaves picked and
　　chopped
finely grated zest of 1 lemon
　　and juice of 2 lemons

Braised octopus
1–1.5 kg cleaned octopus
1 red onion, roughly chopped
1 garlic bulb, peeled
2 celery stalks, roughly
　　chopped
1 carrot, roughly chopped
3 long red chillies, deseeded
　　and roughly chopped
500 ml dry white wine
100 ml white vinegar
　　(or apple cider vinegar)

Preheat the oven to 170°C fan-forced (190°C conventional).

To braise the octopus, place all the ingredients in a roasting tray, mix thoroughly to combine and cover with foil. Place in the oven and cook for about 2 hours. This is one of those cases where the cooking time can be quite variable. Sometimes it's ready after 2 hours, sometimes it's not, and may even need a further 2 hours, depending on how thick the tentacles are. To check, place a knife into a tentacle and if the flesh separates and the cut splits open then you're pretty close. Once cooked, take the octopus out of the tray and place on a cooling rack. Cut into manageable pieces for the barbecue and set aside. Discard the braising liquid.

Preheat the barbecue grill on high.

Heat a medium frying pan over high heat. Add the vegetable oil and once it's nice and hot, add the onion, garlic and chilli. Cook for a minute or two, tossing occasionally, until the onion has softened a little and the garlic is fragrant. Season and set the pan aside.

Toss the octopus in a little olive oil and season. Grill until you see some nice black char lines, turn and repeat on the other side.

Add the grilled octopus to the pan with the onion in it and toss. Add the chopped parsley and lemon zest and juice. Toss through again and serve.

Serves 4

SPICED BARRAMUNDI WITH FENNEL AND HERB SALAD

This may seem like a long list of ingredients with loads of steps. But it's really just whole baked fish with some spices and a fresh little throw-together salad – it's really easy to prepare and a joy to eat. There are many benefits to cooking seafood on the bone: it takes less time to prepare than filleting; the bones will flavour the fish and help to retain the natural juices when cooked; and, importantly, very little goes to waste.

2 teaspoons cumin seeds
2 teaspoons coriander seeds
1 teaspoon whole allspice
2 teaspoons finely grated
    ginger
2 garlic cloves, finely grated
1 long red chilli, finely sliced
3 tablespoons olive oil
2 limes
salt flakes and freshly ground
    pepper
1 small fennel bulb, trimmed
1 small red onion, peeled
1 × 600 g whole barramundi,
    cleaned and scaled
1 small handful of coriander
    leaves, chopped, stalks
    reserved
1 small handful of flat-leaf
    parsley leaves, chopped
1 tablespoon chopped
    roasted almonds

Preheat the oven to 180°C fan-forced (200°C conventional). Tear off a large piece of foil, fold in half – it will need to be roughly the size of the fish with a 5-cm overhang once folded – and place on a baking tray.

Toast the cumin and coriander seeds in a dry frying pan until fragrant and lightly coloured.

Add the toasted spices to a mortar with the allspice, ginger, garlic and half the chilli and grind to a paste. Add one tablespoon of oil and finely grate in the zest of one lime, season and stir to combine.

Cut both the fennel and onion in half, reserve half of each for the salad and cut the remaining halves into three slices each. Arrange the fennel and onion slices along the foil in a line to make a bed for the fish. Drizzle over 1 tablespoon of oil and season.

Slice the barramundi a few times across the fillets on both sides and about halfway to the bone. Rub the spice paste all over the fish, including inside the cavity. Slice the zested lime into four and stuff inside the cavity with the reserved coriander stalks. Place the fish on top of the fennel and onion, pull up the sides of the foil and loosely crimp to hold in the cooking juices, but don't cover the fish or it won't caramelise. Roast for 10 minutes. Carefully turn the fish over and roast for a further 8 minutes or until just cooked.

While the fish is cooking, slice the reserved fennel and onion very finely and add to a bowl with the coriander leaves, parsley, almonds and remaining oil. Squeeze in the other lime, season and toss.

Serve the barramundi with the salad on the side.

Serves 2

BARBECUED PRAWNS WITH CHARRED KALE AND AVOCADO PUREE

We created this dish for the Ballina Prawn Festival, and ended up winning the people's choice award for the prawn dish of the day. It was a forty-four degree day and sticky, busy and pretty smoky standing over those barbecues, and we still couldn't make them fast enough. We're really happy with the way this dish turned out.

1 garlic bulb, peeled
5 long red chillies, deseeded
   and roughly chopped
200 ml olive oil
salt flakes and freshly ground
   pepper
16 large green prawns,
   deveined, shells and
   heads on
1 small handful of flat-leaf
   parsley, leaves picked and
   finely chopped
finely grated zest and juice of
   1 lemon
2 tablespoons vegetable oil
1 large bunch of kale (about
   600 g), leaves stripped and
   roughly chopped

Avocado puree
2 avocados
75 ml buttermilk
juice of ½ lemon
salt flakes and freshly
   ground pepper

Preheat the oven to 160°C fan-forced (180°C conventional).

Add the garlic, chilli, olive oil and plenty of cracked pepper to a small ovenproof saucepan, cover with foil and place in the oven for 1½ hours.

Meanwhile, using a sharp knife, butterfly the prawns by cutting them lengthways along the belly and through the heads until you can open them out flat. Leave the legs on, as they get nice and crunchy once grilled.

For the avocado puree, place the avocado flesh, buttermilk and lemon juice in a food processor and mix on high until smooth. Season to taste and set aside.

Remove the saucepan from the oven. Tip the contents into a food processor and blitz to a paste. Halve the garlic paste, mixing the parsley through one half.

Preheat the barbecue grill and plate on high.

Brush the flesh side of the prawns with the parsley and garlic mix and season well. Grill the prawns flesh side down for a minute or so. Flip and cook for another minute or so until just cooked. They will cook quickly, so be careful. Take the prawns off the grill, sprinkle with the lemon zest and squeeze over the juice.

Drizzle the vegetable oil on the barbecue plate and throw on the kale and the other half of the garlic paste. Season the kale and cook until wilted.

Divide the kale between the plates, stack four prawns on top of each mound of kale, generously dollop some avocado puree on the side and serve.

Serves 4

How to
OPEN AN OYSTER

When prepared properly, oysters are quite possibly the most delicious offerings of the ocean. Pre-shucking oysters, refrigerating them and consuming them hours or even days later is truly doing an injustice to these slippery delights. They must be alive and shucked moments before eating, and are best served chilled and raw. You can steam or deep-fry them, but honestly, why would you? Here is our simple guide to shucking oysters so that you can enjoy them at home.

You'll need:
a good oyster knife
a damp cloth or tea towel
some ice and lemon, to serve

There is a small seam between the top and bottom shells where the hinge is. Press down on the oyster and wiggle the tip of the oyster knife into this seam.

If you imagine the oyster as roughly heart-shaped, at the tip of the heart is a join where the top shell hinges open so that the oyster can feed.

Manoeuvre the handle from side to side with a little downward pressure to pry the shell open. You will hear a pop and feel the top shell come loose.

4

Slide the blade along the right hand side of the shell, applying pressure to the top of the shell so that you don't damage the precious flesh inside.

5

The blade will meet a muscle (which opens and closes the top shell) and once this has been severed the flat top shell of the oyster can be removed.

6

Carefully run the knife along the inside of the shell on the right hand side to cut the same muscle from the bottom shell and release the oyster.

7

Flip the oyster and place it back in the shell, being careful to remove any shell fragments in the process. Serve oysters on ice with wedges of lemon and lime, or try one of the oyster dressings from our first book, *The Blue Ducks*.

CHILLI CRAB

Chilli crab is one of my favourites. It's the dish I cooked for my first date with my girlfriend Hannah, and it worked a treat. Whenever we eat it together, it reminds us both of that exciting time falling in love. Bit mushy, I know, but this dish really brings back great memories. You can pretty much use any crab you like: mud, spanner or blue swimmer. I really like using blue swimmer, as the flesh is a bit sweeter and you can break the shells open with your teeth.

2 blue swimmer crabs
90 g desiccated coconut
juice of 1 lemon
1 red Asian shallot, finely sliced
1 teaspoon chilli flakes
½ bunch of coriander, leaves picked, roots reserved for the chilli mix
vegetable oil, to fry
400 ml coconut milk

Chilli mix
2½ tablespoons vegetable oil
3 red Asian shallots, roughly chopped
4 garlic cloves, roughly chopped
50 g peeled ginger, roughly chopped
6–8-cm lemongrass stalk, white part only, finely chopped
4 long red chillies, roughly chopped
½ bunch of coriander roots, roughly chopped (see above)
60 g palm sugar
2½ tablespoons fish sauce
250 g cherry tomatoes

To make the chilli mix, place a medium saucepan over high heat and add the oil. Once hot, add the shallots, garlic, ginger, lemongrass, chilli and coriander root to the pan while stirring constantly. Everything should start to caramelise pretty quickly. Add the palm sugar, which will melt and make a spicy caramel. Keep cooking until the chillies are soft, add the fish sauce, and continue to cook until the liquid has mostly gone. Add the cherry tomatoes, crushing them with the back of a wooden spoon as you stir. Keep stirring the mix until the tomatoes have completely broken down. Add the mix to a blender and process until smooth, or keep it a bit rough, it's up to you.

Remove the top shell from the crabs, discard the gills and set the mustard aside (only the really yellow parts). Cut each crab into four pieces.

Mix the coconut, lemon juice, sliced shallots and chilli flakes in a small bowl. Tear in the coriander leaves and work into a rough sambal with your fingers.

Place a heavy-based frying pan over high heat, add a splash of oil and heat until shimmering and almost smoking. Add the chilli mix and the reserved mustard from the crab and fry for 1 minute, stirring constantly. Add the crab pieces and coconut milk and cover for a minute or so to bring the liquid to the boil quickly. Once the liquid is at a vigorous boil, remove the lid and cook for 2 minutes – the key here is a quick cooking time, as the meat will start to break down into little pieces if overcooked.

Once cooked, tip the crab into a large bowl along with all the sauce, scatter over a handful of the coconut sambal and serve.

Serves 2

SEARED SQUID WITH FARRO AND CHORIZO SALAD

I know what you're thinking: not more ancient grains! I know they're a bit on-trend at the moment, but forget about all that. Farro, spelt or pearl barley all work an absolute treat with this dish. Apart from being really nutritious and a piece of cake to cook, they soak up the olive oil and citrus juice, and their slightly sweet, nutty flavour and chewy texture is perfect with the squid. It's important with this to get the pan nice and hot, as the squid needs to be fried quickly, otherwise it'll just boil, which isn't good for anyone.

100 g farro
1 blood orange (or navel orange), segmented and the juice squeezed from the remaining membrane
finely grated zest and juice of 1 lime
1 long red chilli, deseeded and finely sliced
200 g cherry tomatoes, halved
1 small red onion, finely sliced
3 tablespoons olive oil
salt flakes and freshly ground pepper
200 g chorizo, thinly sliced
rice bran oil, for frying
500 g cleaned squid, tube cut into 4-cm pieces and tentacles separated and trimmed into short lengths
1 handful of basil leaves, chopped
1 handful of flat-leaf parsley leaves, chopped
1 handful of mint leaves, chopped
1 small handful of rocket
1 small handful of dandelion leaves (optional)

Cook the farro in simmering water for about 45 minutes. Drain, transfer to a large bowl and set aside for 5 minutes to cool.

Once the farro has cooled, add the blood orange, blood orange juice, lime zest and juice, chilli, tomatoes, onion and 2 tablespoons of olive oil, season and toss to combine.

Heat a large frying pan over high heat. Cook the chorizo until it colours slightly and then tip into the farro mix.

Heat the frying pan until it's almost smoking and add a little rice bran oil. Season the squid and cook in batches – if you crowd the pan, the squid will stew and you won't pick up any colour – for about 1 minute or until just cooked. Add the squid to the farro along with the herbs and leaves, drizzle over the remaining olive oil, toss well and serve.

Serves 6

How to
PREPARE & COOK CRAB

Since moving to Byron Bay, catching crabs has become a new pastime for me. The intricate river systems of the mid north coast are jam-packed with fleshy, sweet mud crabs. We head upriver in our trusty Zodiac and drop the crab pots near the muddy riverbanks. The next morning we go back to check them, and more often than not there's a meal or two waiting. Since I started catching mud crabs, I've had the pleasure of talking with local fishermen and hearing their different techniques on how to cook them. Below are three of my favourite methods. Enjoy, but be careful, these guys are extremely addictive. When working with live crabs, it's important that you always chill them in the fridge or freezer until they become still and insensible (non-responsive to stimuli) before you cook them whole or break them down.

The barbecue method

This is quite a brutish method. Fire up the barbecue on high. Place a whole mud crab on the grill and close the hood. Cook for about 10 minutes. When you open the hood you will find a charred, orange crab. Crack the shell open with the back of a heavy knife, squeeze over some lemon, and eat with your fingers.

The chilli sauce method

See the chilli crab recipe on page 114.

The fisherman's boiling method

Place the crab in the sink. On the underside there is a pointy flap that is connected to the carapace (top shell) of the crab.

Add salt to a large saucepan of water until it's about as salty as ocean water and bring to the boil.

Stick your thumb deeply and firmly in behind this pointy flap. Lift and pull in the same motion to remove the carapace.

Remove the gills, as they have a bitter, dirty flavour, but leave most of the orange mustard.

Cut or break the crab in half lengthways.

Using the back of a heavy knife, crack the shells of the two large claws – this just makes it easier to get to the meat once cooked.

Carefully place the crab in the water and, depending on the size, cook for 6–8 minutes.

Lift the crab from the water and rest for 5 minutes. These are wonderful with a citrus and chili mayonnaise.

MUSSELS WITH FREGOLA AND SMOKED PANCETTA

Mussels are great to cook at home as they require very little preparation. This recipe is the sort of food that you could cook for four or forty, and it doesn't really require much more preparation. Just a much bigger pot! This is an absolute no-fuss recipe using an inexpensive and sustainable shellfish. I like to serve it straight from the pot in the middle of the table with large bowls and a ladle, so that guests can help themselves. Some crusty bread and a bottle or two of riesling and you're well set for a cracking night in.

60 ml olive oil
150 g smoked pancetta,
    cut into lardons
3 French shallots, finely sliced
3 garlic cloves, finely sliced
1 long red chilli, finely sliced
200 ml dry white wine
1 tablespoon apple cider
    vinegar
1 teaspoon honey
400 g can diced tomatoes
    (or 400 g overripe
    tomatoes, chopped)
2 thyme sprigs
100 g fregola
2 kg live mussels, de-bearded
1 handful of basil leaves
1 handful of flat-leaf
    parsley leaves
salt flakes and freshly
    ground pepper

Place a wide, heavy-based saucepan over high heat. Once hot, add half the oil and fry the pancetta until crisp. Turn to low–medium heat and add the shallots, garlic and chilli. Sweat without colouring for about 2 minutes, stirring frequently with a wooden spoon. Turn the heat back to high, add the wine, vinegar and honey and cook for 2 minutes, or until the wine has evaporated. Add the tomatoes, thyme and 300 ml of water and simmer for 10–15 minutes.

Add the fregola to the pan and cook for about 10 minutes.

Just before the fregola is ready, add the mussels and quickly stir through. Cover with a lid and cook until the mussels have all opened, about 2–3 minutes. Remove the pan from the heat, scatter over the herbs and drizzle with the remaining oil. Season if necessary and serve immediately with plenty of crusty bread.

Serves 4

FISH, LEEK AND BURNT ONION PIE

I got the idea to burn onions from a brilliant chef, and mate of mine, Dave Pynt. Dave has a restaurant in Singapore called Burnt Ends. Not only is he one of the most positive guys I've ever worked with, he's an absolute gun when it comes to barbecue. He showed me an awesome technique where you place leeks on hot coals and completely blacken them. Once they're charred, you let them cool slightly and peel away the outer layers, leaving you with beautifully cooked smoky leeks. I've adapted the method and used onions for this recipe, which brings a great sweet, smoky quality to the pie. Cheers, Dave!

2 onions, skin on
I leek
700 ml milk
I fresh bay leaf
¼ teaspoon black peppercorns
2 garlic cloves, lightly crushed
400 g white fish fillet
  (snapper, barramundi or
  flathead would all work
  well), skin removed
100 g hot-smoked fish fillet
  (to make your own, see
  page 171)
40 g butter
40 g plain flour
2 tablespoons Dijon mustard
¼ teaspoon ground nutmeg
I teaspoon chopped tarragon
I teaspoon chopped dill
salt flakes and freshly
  ground pepper
I puff pastry sheet
I egg, lightly whisked

Preheat the oven to 180°C fan-forced (200°C conventional). Line a baking tray with baking paper.

Place the onions and leek on the tray and roast for 30 minutes.

After 30 minutes, remove the leek and set aside. Turn the oven up to 200°C fan-forced (220°C conventional) and roast the onions for a further 30 minutes – they should look burnt once done. Once cool, trim the leek and onions and remove the outer layers. Chop the flesh into 4-cm chunks.

Reduce the oven to 180°C fan-forced (200°C conventional).

To poach the fish, place the milk, bay leaf, peppercorns, garlic and white fish in a medium saucepan over low heat. When the milk is just ticking over, cook very gently for 6–8 minutes. Lift the fish out of the milk and flake into a bowl, being careful to remove any bones. Flake the smoked fish into the same bowl. Strain and reserve the poaching milk.

To make the sauce, melt the butter in a medium saucepan over medium heat. Add the flour and stir constantly for about 1½ minutes to cook out the raw flour flavour. Slowly pour the reserved poaching milk into the pan while whisking constantly. Once smooth, stir with a wooden spoon until thickened. Remove from the heat and set aside to cool to room temperature.

Once the sauce has cooled, add the mustard, nutmeg and herbs and season with salt and loads of pepper. Add the fish, leek and onion to the sauce and mix through very gently, keeping the fish in large flakes. Transfer the mix to a 1.4-litre baking dish. Cover the dish with the puff pastry, crimp lightly to seal and trim off any excess. Make a couple of incisions in the pastry to release some steam and brush with egg. Bake for 20–25 minutes until the pastry is golden.

Serves 6

OVEN-ROASTED SCALLOPS WITH LIME AND HERB BUTTER

Scallops are still a bit of a luxury, but when they're in season, they're affordable and delicious. Local green or white asparagus is great for this recipe, but if asparagus is out of season just opt for something else: leeks, green onion, salsify or diced potatoes with hazelnuts will all work really well. Try to avoid buying imported vegetables, if something is local and in season it honestly can't be beat.

6 asparagus spears
60 g butter, at room
   temperature
1 teaspoon soy sauce
finely grated zest and juice
   of ½ lime
1 handful of chervil leaves,
   chopped
1 handful of flat-leaf parsley
   leaves, chopped
salt flakes and freshly
   ground pepper
1 pinch of finely grated garlic
4 scallops in their shells

Preheat the oven to 185°C fan-forced (205°C conventional). Fill a medium bowl with ice and water to refresh the asparagus in.

Cook the asparagus in boiling salted water for 1–2 minutes (depending on the thickness of the spears) until just cooked, and then refresh in the iced water. Cut on an angle into 2-mm thick slices.

Whisk the butter in a medium bowl. Add the soy, lime zest and herbs, season and add the garlic, but go easy, as it can be overpowering. Whisk until combined.

Top each scallop with the asparagus and then the lime butter and bake for 2–3 minutes – the butter will melt over the asparagus and the scallops should be just cooked. Squeeze over the lime juice and serve.

Serves 4

MEAT
& POULTRY

GOOD OLD ROAST CHOOK

Good gravy goes a long way, bad gravy reminds me of the RSL. Don't get me wrong, I love the 'Ari', but I'm yet to have gravy in one that has blown my socks off. When you're making this, there will be some dark sticky bits in the roasting tray that look just irresistible. But try to resist! These bits of sticky goodness are what will put your gravy in the hall of fame. If gravy's not your thing, cook the chook on a wire rack with a tray of veg underneath to baste in the juices.

1 × 1.6–1.8 kg chicken,
  removed from the fridge
  an hour before cooking
80 g butter
2 garlic cloves, sliced
salt flakes and freshly ground
  pepper
1 good pinch of smoked
  paprika
1 lemon

Gravy
1 tablespoon plain flour
1 tablespoon tomato paste
50 ml port
200 ml red wine
salt flakes and freshly
  ground pepper

Preheat the oven to 200°C fan-forced (220°C conventional).

Working from the cavity up, slide your fingers between the skin and the breast of the chicken to create pockets for the butter and garlic – the breast meat is the first to cook on a chicken, so we need to work harder to keep it moist. Slide the butter and garlic under the skin of each breast. Season the chicken heavily – the salt will help make the skin crispy – place in a roasting tray and roast for 20 minutes. This will give the skin a chance to crisp up and help to lock in some of the juices.

After 20 minutes, turn the oven down to 180°C fan-forced (200°C conventional). Sprinkle paprika over the bird and roast for another 35–40 minutes.

To check the chicken, pull the leg away from the side of the bird and slice it down to the bone where it joins the torso. If it's still a little pink and bloody, it needs a bit longer. Cooking time will depend on the size of the chicken, the oven's ability to hold temperature, and, to a certain degree, the type of chicken you buy. Once cooked, remove from the tray and rest on a board while you make the gravy.

Take the roasting tray and place it over low heat on the stovetop. Add the flour and tomato paste and cook for a minute or so while stirring. Deglaze with the port and half the red wine, incorporating all the caramelised bits from the tray into the gravy with your spoon. Use the remainder of the wine to adjust the thickness of the gravy, season and pour into a gravy boat.

Carve the chicken, squeeze over a little lemon juice and serve with generous portions of gravy.

Serves 4–6

RISSOLES ... IT'S WHAT YOU DO WITH THEM!

The humble beef rissole is the staple of every Australian barbecue. Let's be honest, done well or well done, they still taste alright – even the next day. People swear by their rissole recipes. Some are partial to a traditional plain rissole, but I like to add a whole bunch of dried fruit, pine nuts and parsley to mine. This recipe has served me well at many a barbie. Serve with tomato sauce, pasta salad, potato salad, a cheeky lamb chop and a sausage sanga. Can't get much more Australian than that.

1 kg prime beef mince
200 g panko (or sourdough breadcrumbs)
200 g currants
150 g pine nuts, toasted
4 eggs
3 handfuls of flat-leaf parsley, leaves picked and roughly chopped
1 large red onion, finely chopped
2 tablespoons minced garlic
75 ml kecap manis
2 tablespoons chilli flakes
2 tablespoons smoked paprika
1 tablespoon salt flakes
2 teaspoons ground pepper

Preheat the barbecue grill on high.

Mix all the ingredients in a large bowl until well combined. Roll the mix into rissoles of your preferred shape and size.

Grill the rissoles for 3–5 minutes on each side, depending on how big you make them. Rest for 10 minutes covered with foil before serving.

Serves 4–6

THE GOODNESS OF
Broths & Stocks

DARREN: As a young chef, one of the first things I was responsible for were the stocks. Every day I'd have to make 20 litres of chicken stock for the other chefs to use as the base of risottos, soups and sauces – it was a bit of pressure for a young lad. It's such a simple thing, cooking bones, vegetables, herbs and spices in water, but with a little care, you're left with a rich, nourishing and flavoursome liquid.

Stocks and bone broths are primitive and traditional foods that have been consumed across the globe for centuries – in Xi'an, in the Shaanxi province of China, a team of archaeologists recently unearthed a bronze cauldron of bone soup that they believe is 2,400 years old. Broths and stocks are inexpensive to make and incredibly nutritious.

Bone broths and stocks start out in the same way: bones, meat, vegetables and herbs simmered in water. As they cook, the water is skimmed and, eventually, the liquid is strained to remove the solids. The real difference between them is in the cooking time.

Bone broth is simmered for a long time, often over 24 hours. This releases minerals from the cooking bones as well as collagen and gelatine from connective tissue, joints and tendons. When the bone broth is finally cooked, the bones will crumble under pressure between your fingers. See overleaf for our beef bone broth recipe.

Stock is simmered for a shorter amount of time, usually about 3–4 hours.

BONE BROTHS ARE GELATINOUS, NUTRIENT-DENSE ELIXIRS

- They are incredibly high in protein as well as calcium, phosphorous, magnesium and other trace minerals that strengthen our immune systems.
- They attract digestive juices to the gut, restoring the mucosal lining of the stomach and supporting digestion.
- They are detoxifying.
- They are gelatine-rich for healthy joints, nails, skin and hair.

TIPS FOR YOUR STOCKS AND BONE BROTHS

- Roast the bones beforehand, as this adds incredible flavour.
- Throw in some chicken feet for added collagen and gelatine.
- Don't be afraid! Use knuckles, necks and hocks – the more cartilaginous the better. Add some vinegar, citrus juice or any kind of acid to your broth. This will help to leach minerals from the bones as they cook.
- Make them a regular part of your diet. Cook up big batches and freeze. Use bone broth as the base of soup, risotto and braises or just enjoy on their own.

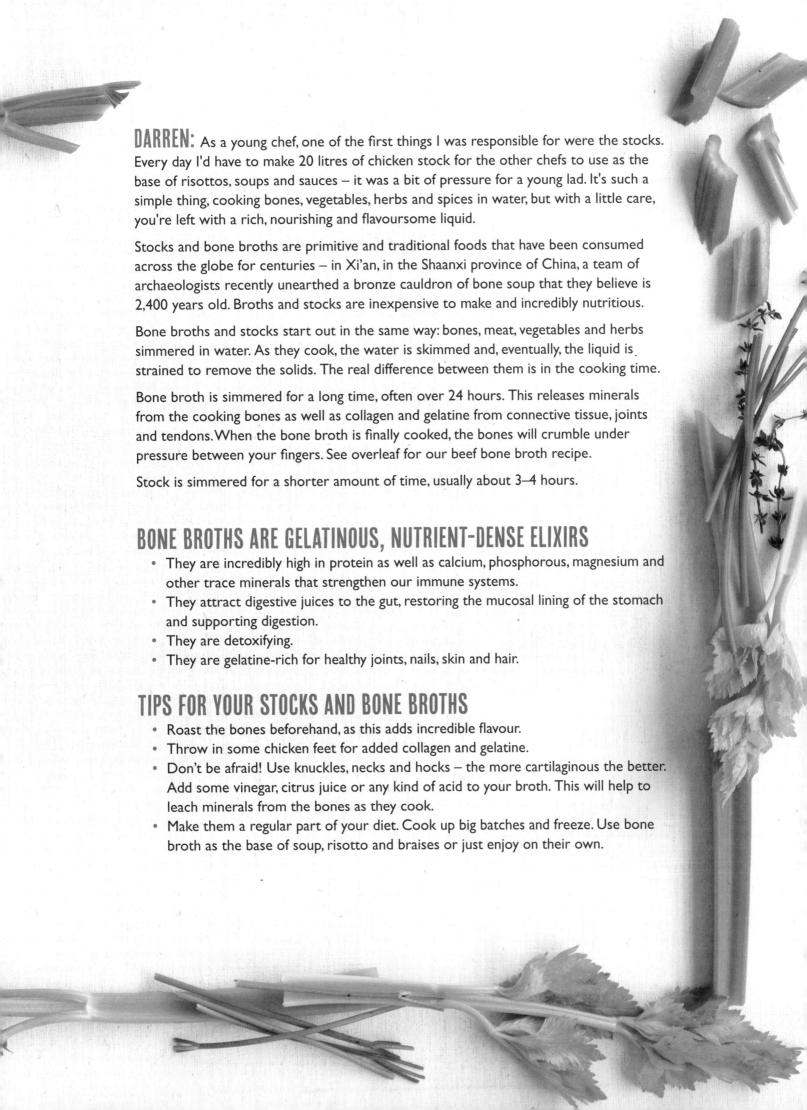

BEEF BONE BROTH

A bone broth is a basic meal, but its health benefits are incredible. The process of slow-cooking bones and tendons creates a nutrient-rich elixir. The benefits of bone broth include: promotion of gut health; increased immunity; reduced pain and inflammation in joints; collagen-rich skin, hair and nails; and strengthened bones. Make big batches of bone broth, store in your freezer and drink it at least once a week as you would a cup of tea or some soup. Ask your butcher for marrow-dense bones such as shanks, the more gristly and gnarly looking the better.

4 kg beef bones
5 chicken feet
2 onions, roughly chopped
6 garlic cloves, peeled
½ celeriac, roughly chopped
2 carrots, roughly chopped
1 fennel bulb, roughly chopped
5 celery stalks, roughly chopped
4-cm piece of ginger, roughly
   chopped
1 tablespoon black peppercorns
125 ml apple cider vinegar
1 large handful of flat-leaf
   parsley, leaves picked and
   stalks reserved

Place all the ingredients except the parsley leaves (but including the stalks) in a large saucepan and fill with about 10 litres of water (purified or filtered, if possible). Place over high heat and bring up to a simmer. Turn the heat to low, and skim any scum or foam from the stock as it forms. Cook very gently for 24 hours, topping up with a little more water as needed.

Strain the stock and serve with a sprinkling of chopped parsley. A thin layer of fat will form on the surface of the liquid as it cools, but don't be alarmed, as this is also good for you. Whatever you don't use can be refrigerated for a couple of days, or frozen for a couple of months.

Makes 7–8 litres

ASIAN-STYLE CHICKEN SOUP

There's a reason why your grandmother used to tell you to eat chicken soup when you were sick: besides being warming and flavourful, it's also incredibly nutrient dense. Here is my take, with Asian flavours – there's nothing like a bit of chilli to clear the sinuses.

1 × 1.6–1.8 kg chicken
6 garlic cloves, chopped
4-cm piece of ginger, chopped
2 lemongrass stems, bottom
   two-thirds only, cut into
   10-cm lengths
1 red onion, roughly chopped
1 carrot, roughly chopped
1 long red chilli, chopped
1 bunch of coriander, leaves
   picked and finely chopped,
   stalks roughly chopped
soy sauce, to taste

Add the chicken, garlic, ginger, lemongrass, onion, carrot, chilli and coriander stalks to a large saucepan. Fill with 5 litres of water (purified or filtered, if possible) and bring to the boil. Reduce to a simmer and cook for 2½ hours.

Once cooked, carefully lift the chicken out of the broth and set aside on a tray to cool – be careful, it will be very fragile. Strain the broth (all the bits in the strainer can go straight in the compost) into a clean saucepan.

Once the chicken is cool enough to handle, pick all the meat from the bones and shred. Warm the broth and add the shredded chicken. Season with soy sauce, add the chopped coriander and serve.

Serves 4–6

SLOW-COOKED BEEF CHEEKS ON SOFT POLENTA

We had these cheeks on the menu during our first season in the snow. They're perfect after a day on the slopes. We served them with a burnt potato puree, but they're also stunning with soft polenta and some quick pickles. Try not to be put off by the amount of time it takes to cook the cheeks. They are full of collagen, which needs to be slowly broken down, but once it has, you're left with succulent, delicate and flavoursome meat that just melts in the mouth.

2 tablespoons vegetable oil
6 × 200 g beef cheeks
salt flakes and freshly
 ground pepper
500 ml red wine
500 ml vegetable stock (or
 water)
400 g can diced tomatoes
60 g tomato paste
8 garlic cloves, sliced
1 long red chilli, chopped
3 fresh bay leaves
2 teaspoons smoked paprika
2 cinnamon sticks
1 red onion
juice of 1 lime
1 lemon
1 handful of flat-leaf parsley
 leaves

Soft polenta
1 litre vegetable stock
 (or water)
200 ml fine instant polenta
40 g butter
50 g parmesan, finely grated
2 teaspoons lemon juice
salt flakes and freshly
 ground pepper

Preheat the oven to 180°C fan-forced (200°C conventional).

Heat a heavy-based ovenproof pan over medium–high heat and add the vegetable oil. Season the beef cheeks and brown all over for about 5 minutes. Remove the cheeks and set aside on a plate.

In the same pan, bring the red wine, stock, tomatoes, tomato paste, garlic, chilli, bay leaves and spices to a boil. Add the beef cheeks back to the pan, along with any juices on the plate, and add enough water to just cover. Seal with foil or a lid and cook for 3 hours. Once cooked, the meat will be soft to the touch.

While the cheeks braise, trim the top of the onion but leave the root intact. Place the onion on your board, cut-end down, and slice into six wedges. Trim the root off each of the wedges, peel and separate the layers of onion to make petals. Blanch the onion petals in boiling salted water for 30 seconds and then refresh in iced water. Dry the onion with paper towel and pickle in the lime juice for 30 minutes.

Very carefully remove the beef cheeks from the pan and set aside. Skim any fat off the braising liquid and reduce on the stovetop by about half. Adjust the seasoning, squeeze in lemon juice to taste, and return the cheeks to the pan.

For the soft polenta, bring the stock to the boil and whisk in the polenta over medium heat. Stir for 2–3 minutes until smooth. Remove from the heat and stir in the butter, parmesan and lemon juice. Season to taste.

Serve the beef cheeks and sauce on the polenta with a scattering of onion petals and parsley leaves over the top.

Serves 6

HOME-STYLE BRISKET WITH COFFEE SPICE RUB

I do like brisket. Like, a lot. It's the ultimate barbecue cut. Biting into a slice of brisket that's been smoked overnight is life changing. It's almost a religion in the American South, and people spend lifetimes perfecting recipes. But don't be intimidated by it; the trick with brisket is to cook it low and slow. And try to marinate the meat overnight if you can — it makes a real difference.

1 × 1.5 kg brisket
1 quantity Coffee Spice Rub
(see page 93)
1 tablespoon vegetable oil

Sprinkle about a third of the spice rub over the brisket, making sure it's well coated, and massage into the meat. The leftover spice rub can be stored in an airtight jar for another time. Refrigerate the brisket overnight, or for at least a good 4 hours, to allow the spices to flavour the meat.

Preheat the oven to 150°C fan-forced (170°C conventional).

When ready to cook, pour the oil and 40 ml of water into a roasting tray and slosh it around to coat the base of the tray. Besides making the washing up easier, the water will help steam the meat and keep it nice and moist. Place the brisket in the tray, cover very tightly with foil and cook for 4–5 hours. Once cooked, the brisket will be soft to the touch and will feel like you can almost push a finger though it. Rest for 15 minutes before slicing and serving.

This is great with chimichurri and slaw, in a taco, in a sandwich with hot barbecue sauce and pickles, or with corn or baked potatoes.

Serves 6

KANGAROO TARTARE WITH BRIK PASTRY

Kangaroo is something we should all be eating. It's an incredibly lean meat, super sustainable and very reasonably priced. This dish is one we serve in Bronte, and we really enjoy making it, it's really tasty and looks great too. I recommend serving this as an entree, as a couple of hundred grams of raw meat can be a bit confronting. We love serving this with shards of crispy brik pastry, but if you don't have time to make these, simply use toasted brioche or sourdough fried in a little duck fat instead. Look for brik pastry at Middle Eastern grocers or specialty food stores.

500 g kangaroo fillet
3 cornichons, finely diced
1 tablespoon capers, finely chopped
4 French shallots, finely diced
1 small handful of flat-leaf parsley, leaves picked and finely chopped
1 bunch of chives, finely chopped
salt flakes and freshly ground pepper
nasturtium leaves and flowers (optional)

Sauce
3 egg yolks
260 g tomato sauce
110 g Dijon mustard
3 teaspoons Worcestershire sauce
3 teaspoons Tabasco
salt flakes and freshly ground pepper

Brik pastry with olive tapenade
2 sheets of brik pastry
2 tablespoons good-quality olive tapenade

To make the brik pastry with olive tapenade, preheat the oven to 190°C.

Take 1 sheet of brik pastry and lay it on a piece of baking paper. Smear the pastry with 1 tablespoon of the olive tapenade and place another piece of baking paper on top. Place on a baking tray and add another baking tray on top, making sure the baking paper and pastry is pressed firmly between the two trays – this will ensure the pastry stays flat when baked. Bake for 15 minutes, or until the pastry is nice and crispy. Repeat this process with the second sheet of brik pastry and remaining olive tapenade. Once cool, break the pastry into shards and set aside until ready to serve.

Next, finely dice the kangaroo fillet. Take some care doing this, and don't do it too far ahead of time. It's important that the tartare is served cold, so put the diced meat back in the fridge to chill before assembling.

To make the sauce, combine all the ingredients in a medium bowl and season to taste.

To make the tartare, add the kangaroo, cornichons, capers, shallots, parsley and chives to a large bowl and mix well. Add the sauce gradually until dressed to your liking – personally, I like my tartare quite wet, but it's up to you. Season well (kangaroo can take a good amount of pepper).

Spoon the tartare onto a platter, scatter over some nasturtium leaves and flowers (if using) and serve immediately with the brik pastry.

Serves 4

TANDOORI-STYLE BARBECUED QUAIL

These little guys are tasty, addictive and pretty fun to make. And if you ever wondered why Indian chefs have orange hands, you're about to find out! These are traditionally cooked in a tandoor, which is about as hot as a jet engine at full blast. It's a deep vertical tube made of clay, and brave tandoor chefs put their entire arms inside to stick the meat to the wall. Once the meat is cooked, it falls away from the sides, resulting in an amazing product – and a chef with no arm hair. This dish needs to be eaten with your hands – it's a crime if you don't!

250 g tandoori paste (Indian grocers will sell authentic imports or, if you're keen, make it from scratch)
350 g natural yoghurt
8 quail, butterflied
vegetable oil, for grilling
salt flakes and freshly ground pepper
lime wedges, to serve

Yoghurt dressing
200 g natural yoghurt
1 cucumber, deseeded and grated
1 young garlic bulb (or 2 large garlic cloves), finely sliced
3 spring onions, finely sliced
finely grated zest and juice of ½ lemon
1 large handful of mint, leaves picked and finely chopped
1 teaspoon ground cumin
1 teaspoon chilli powder
salt flakes and freshly ground pepper

To make the marinade, combine the tandoori paste and yoghurt in a large bowl. Add the quail and mix by hand until the birds are well coated – be careful with the quail when you do this, as they are quite fragile. Set aside to marinate for a few hours. This is best done on the bench rather than in the fridge.

Preheat the barbecue grill on high.

To make the yoghurt dressing, combine all the ingredients in a medium bowl and season to taste.

Dip a clean cloth in oil and rub it quickly along the grill bars – be careful as it may flame. Carefully place the quail, skin-side down, on the grill and cook for 2 minutes. Flip and cook for another 2 minutes. Season the quail as it comes off the grill and set aside in a warm place. Rest for a good 8 minutes to finish the cooking and relax the meat.

Serve the quail with a good drizzle of the yoghurt dressing and lime wedges.

Serves 4

STICKY BRAISED BEEF SHIN

This really is a 'throw it together, lid on' recipe. You only really need to take a little care when colouring the shin before braising. I like to serve this with our cucumber and chilli salad (see page 35) and a bowl of steamed jasmine rice.

1.5 kg beef shin, cut into
  5-cm slices
1 tablespoon Five-Spice Salt
  (see page 23)
1 tablespoon vegetable oil

Braising liquid
1 litre beef stock
500 ml shaoxing wine
  (Chinese cooking wine)
2 tablespoons soy sauce
1½ tablespoons oyster sauce
1 tablespoon fish sauce
1 tablespoon honey
3 garlic cloves
4-cm piece of ginger, sliced
1 long red chilli, split

Season the beef with the five spice mix and ideally set aside for a good 4 hours – the salt in the five spice mix will draw moisture from the beef and, given enough time, will send the flavour of the spices deep into the meat.

Preheat the oven to 170°C fan-forced (190°C conventional).

Heat the oil in a large ovenproof pan over medium–high heat. Add the beef and caramelise on all sides. Take a bit of time doing this, as it really improves the end result; the more colour you get on the beef, without burning it, the better. Add all the braising ingredients, cover with foil or a lid and cook for 2–2½ hours.

Once cooked, the meat will be soft to the touch. Remove the pan from the oven, carefully lift the meat from the liquid and set aside. Place the pan back over medium heat and reduce the sauce until sticky and thick enough to coat the back of a spoon. Add the meat back to the pan and take it directly to the table.

Serve the beef with jasmine rice and our cucumber and chilli salad (see page 35).

Serves 6

MELTINGLY GOOD SLOW-COOKED PORK

After I left Tetsuya's, I rented a little commercial kitchen from a Portuguese couple. Every Friday I used to cook pork shoulders overnight to sell in buns with beetroot, kohlrabi slaw and hot sauce at farmer's markets the next day. As much as I wasn't a fan of the early mornings, I do miss the good old days driving to the markets, music blaring and coffee in hand, hoping that I'd return with an empty van. This is the kind of food that's great with loads of salads, slaw, hot sauce and plenty of cold beers. And if you have leftovers, just turn it into pulled pork. Try this with the herb and apple slaw on page 37.

P.S. Wayne and Fatty, cheers for letting me use the kitchen!

1.6 kg boned pork shoulder, skin removed
salt flakes
2 tablespoons vegetable oil
6 Dutch cream potatoes, scrubbed

Marinade
1 tablespoon coriander seeds
2 tablespoons grapeseed oil
2 tablespoons honey
2 tablespoons soy sauce
1 tablespoon fish sauce
2 garlic cloves, finely grated
2 teaspoons chilli powder

Preheat the oven to 150°C fan-forced (170°C conventional).

Make about ten incisions in the pork to help the marinade penetrate the meat. Season the shoulder with salt. Place a large ovenproof pan over medium–high heat and add the vegetable oil. Once hot, sear the meat for about 5 minutes on each side until golden brown. Remove from the pan and set aside for 5 minutes.

For the marinade, toast the coriander seeds in a dry frying pan until fragrant and lightly coloured.

Using a mortar and pestle, grind the coriander seeds to a powder. Add to a small bowl with the other marinade ingredients and combine.

Massage the marinade into the pork and return to the pan with the potatoes and 500 ml of water. Cover with foil or a lid, place in the oven and cook for 4–5 hours. Once cooked, the meat will be soft to the touch, and the potatoes will be tender and full of flavour from the cooking juices. Rest for 15 minutes before serving.

Serve the pork with the potatoes, some juices from the pan and slaw on the side.

Shred any leftover pork into a bowl and pour in the remaining cooking juices to make pulled pork.

Serves 6

BRAISED LAMB SHOULDER – THE ONE POT WONDER

Let me take some of the wonder out of this easy dish. Just put everything in a pot and cook for three hours. It's close to impossible to ruin this. It's the perfect set-and-forget dish, put it on and head out for a solid surf session, and when you return, that insatiable hunger will be met with a hearty, fall-off-the-bone lamb shoulder. Serve with wet polenta or crusty bread.

1 × 2–2.5 kg lamb shoulder, bone in
salt flakes and freshly ground pepper
2 tablespoons vegetable oil
1 handful of cocktail onions, peeled
1 bulb of garlic, peeled
2 carrots, peeled and chopped into chunks
2 long red chillies, roughly chopped
3 heaped tablespoons tomato paste
750 ml red wine
1 litre vegetable stock (or chicken stock)
6–8 sprigs of rosemary, leaves picked and roughly chopped
1 handful of thyme sprigs, leaves picked and roughly chopped
400 g can diced tomatoes
10–12 chat potatoes

Preheat the barbecue grill on high.

Heavily season the lamb shoulder and grill until it's coloured and a little charred on each side. Set the lamb aside.

Place a heavy-based saucepan, large enough to hold the lamb with the lid on, over high heat. Add the oil, onions, garlic, carrot and chilli and fry, stirring, until the onions take on a little colour. Add the tomato paste and fry until really caramelised – the tomato paste will darken and the pan will start to get quite sticky. Deglaze with the red wine and stock. Add the rosemary, thyme and tomatoes, stir, and then add the lamb to the pan. Throw in the potatoes and bring to a simmer with the lid on. Turn the heat down to low, season and cook very gently for 3 hours – you want the liquid to just tick over, if you lose too much liquid to evaporation you won't end up with a beautiful, tender piece of lamb.

Once cooked, you can serve straight from the pan or transfer the lamb and potatoes to a serving platter and spoon over the braising liquid – reduced if you prefer. Serve with wet polenta or crusty bread.

Serves 6

FLANK STEAK TARTARE WITH PICKLED CARROTS AND SALSA VERDE

This is a great little entree, snack or canapé. If you ferment your own carrots, brilliant, otherwise this quick pickle does the job. A really good flank steak lends itself well to this dish. Flank is easy to slice, as you can use the grain of the meat as a guide, it's less expensive than eye fillet and has more flavour. For a bit more kick, try grating some fresh horseradish over the top. Serve with thinly sliced sourdough toast rubbed with garlic and drizzled with olive oil.

2 tablespoons white
   wine vinegar
I teaspoon caster sugar
salt flakes and freshly
   ground pepper
2 Dutch carrots, peeled and
   finely sliced on a mandoline
240 g flank steak, cut into
   3-mm dice
2 tablespoons chopped
   French shallots

Salsa verde
3 tablespoons chopped
   carrot tops (leaves,
   no stalks)
I large handful of basil,
   leaves picked (reserve a
   few leaves for garnish)
I large handful of flat-leaf
   parsley, leaves picked
   (reserve a few leaves for
   garnish)
I small garlic clove, chopped
I tablespoon capers
I anchovy fillet
3 tablespoons olive oil
juice of ½ lemon
salt flakes and freshly
   ground pepper

To pickle the carrots, combine the vinegar, sugar and a pinch of salt in a small bowl. Add the carrots, toss and set aside for 20 minutes to pickle.

To make the salsa verde, use a mortar and pestle to smash all the ingredients, except the oil and lemon juice, to make a paste. Slowly mix in the olive oil and lemon juice and season to taste.

Add the diced meat to a medium bowl with the shallots, 3 tablespoons of salsa (or to taste), the pickled carrots and I teaspoon of the pickling liquid, season and combine.

Arrange the meat on four small plates and add a little more of the salsa. Scatter over the reserved basil and parsley leaves and serve with toasted sourdough on the side.

Serves 4 as an entree

OUR BLOOD CAKE

We had this dish on our first ever Three Blue Ducks dinner menu. It's been with us for some time, so it has a bit of sentimental value. Cooking with fresh pig's blood probably isn't for everyone, but if you're keen and can get hold of some from your local butcher, try this, it's an absolute treat. Pan-fry slices of the blood cake until crisp on the outside and creamy and rich, but still delicately textured, in the middle. We often serve ours for dinner with a pickled beetroot, shallot and parsley salad and a fried duck egg. It's also beautiful for breakfast, with fried eggs, some sliced red onion and apple, parsley leaves and a little lemon juice squeezed over top. This recipe can be halved.

200 ml cream
40 g sourdough bread, crusts removed, blitzed to a coarse crumb
130 g raw sugar
1 beetroot, peeled and cut into 5-mm dice
1½ tablespoons rice wine vinegar
2 granny smith apples, peeled and cut into 5-mm dice
380 g lardo, cut into 5-mm dice
2 red onions, peeled and finely diced
1 tablespoon Chinese five-spice
700 ml fresh pig's blood
salt flakes and freshly ground pepper

Preheat the oven to 140°C fan-forced (160°C conventional). Line a large casserole or baking dish with baking paper.

Puree the cream and breadcrumbs in a blender.

Add the sugar to a non-stick frying pan and place over high heat. Once the sugar has turned to a medium-coloured caramel, add the beetroot and vinegar and cook for 2 minutes, shaking the pan to coat and combine. Mix in the apple and remove from the heat.

Boil a full kettle.

Melt about a fifth of the lardo in a medium saucepan. Add the onion and soften without colouring for a couple of minutes. Add the five-spice, cream and bread puree, and the blood. Turn the heat down to low and cook for a minute or two, stirring constantly, until the mix thickens slightly. Pour in the apple and beetroot caramel and remaining lardo. Ideally it needs to be thick enough so that the lardo, beetroot and apple don't sink to the bottom of the pan (you can test this first with a piece of apple). Adjust the seasoning if necessary – it mightn't need any more salt, as the lardo should add a fair bit, but grind in some pepper.

Pour the mix into the prepared dish and place the dish in a deep roasting tray. Pour the boiling water into the tray to create a water bath and place in the oven for about 20 minutes. Once cooked, the blood cake should still have a slight wobble to it.

Remove the dish from the water bath and set aside to cool. Wrap in plastic wrap and refrigerate until firm before using.

Makes 1.2 kg

PRESERVING
FOOD

While traditional preserving methods seem counterintuitive – turning food into bubbling, fizzing and sometimes mouldy jars of bacteria – it is exactly this transformation that makes them so utterly delicious.

By its very nature, food begins to spoil the minute that it's harvested. Whether picked from a tree, pulled from the ground, milked from an animal, or slaughtered, food immediately starts to decay. Various techniques have been developed over time to treat or handle food in such a way as to retard spoiling, while also maintaining nutritional value, texture and flavour.

For ancient cultures, creating methods of food preservation meant that they were no longer forced to eat their food immediately, but rather could preserve some of the bounty for later. The techniques remain exactly the same today. The only difference between the way ancient cultures preserved their food and the way we do it today is that now we don't preserve because we have to, we preserve because we want to. Brillat-Savarin famously said: 'Tell me what you eat, and I will tell you what you are.' What we eat is a reflection of so many things – including ethnicity, nationality and culture – and understanding what our ancestors ate illuminates the connection between food traditions and our own histories.

There are many incentives for using traditional methods of preserving food: for the home cook, it's a way of increasing the intake of nutrient-rich food while saving money; for the home gardener, it's a way of value-adding to their seasonal produce by extending the life of their more abundant crops; for the chef, it provides interesting and nuanced flavours and textures, and is a great way of saving produce before it spoils. At the Ducks, we preserve food in season so that we can enjoy it out of season. Some of our favourite methods of preserving are: drying, fermenting, smoking, pickling and making preserves. We use these techniques constantly when experimenting with dishes.

The key to experimenting with these food preservation methods is in understanding the power of transformation over time – microbial, flavour and textural changes. When dealing with live foods, the process of transformation carries on without you. If you leave some freshly picked cucumbers in brine, they will soften and become tangy and sour. If left alone, a cup of kombucha that tastes sweet and refreshing one day, will taste vinegary and pungent three weeks later. It's a whole new game of understanding flavour complexity. For example, last year Mark made a drink of fresh lemon juice, ginger juice and honey. He sampled it and immediately named it the Lemsip because it tasted like a cough lolly: acidic and bitter with a tannic aftertaste. As an experiment, he left it alone for 8 months, and when sampled after its hibernation, it tasted unbelievable. The flavours had mellowed out and meshed, and it had ripened into an entirely different drink. Sometimes, it's just about giving the ingredients time to react with one another and mature.

Many recipes in this chapter require sterilised jars. We like to use recycled glass jars (not plastic) with tight-fitting lids. First, wash them well in very hot, soapy water, then rinse well in hot water. Next, if you have a dishwasher, put the jars and lids in the machine and run it on the hot rinse cycle (it needs to reach 80°C). This should kill most of the bacteria lurking in the jars. If you don't have a dishwasher, place the jars in a large saucepan or stockpot, cover with water and bring to the boil over high heat. Boil for 10 minutes, then place the jars upside down on clean tea towels to drain.

DRYING

Drying is the most ancient food preservation technique, and was used by prehistoric humans because of the way it removes the moisture required for bacteria, yeast and mould growth. Traditionally, drying was carried out by harnessing the power of the world's largest natural dehydrator: the sun. Today, you can simply purchase a dehydrator or just use your oven. Think fleshy pieces of beef jerky, tangy dried apricots and raw popcorn.

Some tips for drying fruit and vegetables:
- Use fresh, fully ripened fruit and vegetables – drying doesn't work well with young or green produce.
- Wash the produce to remove dirt and pesticides.
- Pre-treating the produce stops fruit from going dark and speeds the drying time by helping to break down fruit with tough skins, like plums and cherries. Create a pre-treatment solution made up of 2 teaspoons of citric acid or lemon juice, or 5 tablespoons of ascorbic acid, per litre of water, and soak the produce for 10 minutes. Drain well before drying.
- If drying in the sun, place the produce on a baking tray and leave in direct sunlight.
- If drying in an oven, place the produce on a baking tray and dry at 60°C. The length of time required will depend on the size of the pieces being dried, the humidity and the amount of air circulating within the oven. To give you an idea, we usually dry apple slices for around 5 hours, but a good indicator is when the produce is leathery and malleable. Some vegetables, however, will go hard and brittle, which is normal too.
- Once the produce is dry, allow it to condition for 4–10 days before storing. To condition, allow the dried produce to cool and then pack it loosely in sealed containers. Shake the containers daily. Conditioning equalises the moisture and stops mould developing, as the excess moisture in some pieces is absorbed by the drier pieces.
- After conditioning, pack in containers, seal tightly and store in a cool, dark and dry place.
- Eat dried food within 6–12 months.

See page 164 for a recipe for kimchi chips; page 167 for cavolo nero crisps; page 168 for smoked paprika and lime jerky; page 23 for citrus salt, chilli salt and olive and basil salt; and page 166 for pineapple, mango and lime sherbet.

FERMENTING

Fermentation is all about the joy of eating decaying matter. I bet you love decaying matter too. If you've ever indulged in yoghurt, cheese, sourdough bread, wine, beer, miso or sauerkraut, then you've eaten fermented food.

Fermentation produces lactic acid, alcohol and acetic acid, which are bio-preservatives and act to stop the food from perishing and help to retain nutrients. More than that, fermentation breaks the nutrients down into more digestible, bioavailable forms. For example, olives are stone fruit that are mostly inedible until fermented. Fermentation converts the olive's natural sugars into lactic acid, and breaks down their bitter chemical compounds. Fermentation also creates new nutrients, including B vitamins, antioxidants, omega-3 fatty acids, digestive enzymes, lactase and lactic acid. Fermented foods strengthen immunity, detoxify, increase alkalinity in the gut, and supply the digestive system with live cultures that are essential for breaking down food and absorbing nutrients. If you are buying commercially available fermented foods, however, look at the label to see if they're pasteurised. Pasteurisation heats food to a temperature at which microorganisms, including the treasured good bacteria, die. To avoid this, and have complete control over the process of fermentation, including flavour and texture, ferment your own foods!

The taste of homemade ferments can walk a fine line between delicious food and spoilt goods, depending on how long you leave them to ferment. A good example is kimchi. When you start eating your own kimchi, you might prefer the taste of it after only 4–5 days. However, as your palate adjusts, you might find yourself favouring a more intense 10-day ferment. Our best advice? Have a play.

Just about any food can be fermented. Considering that, rather than attempting to describe the almost

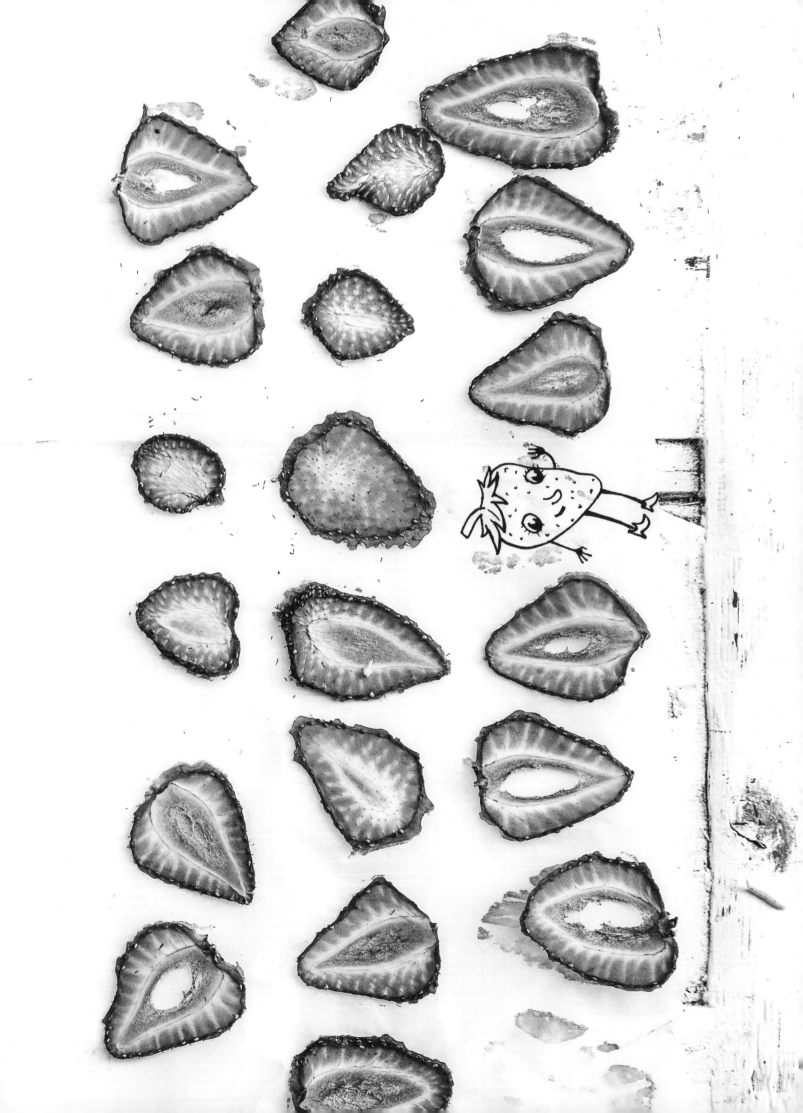

limitless fermentation permutations of every food, here are some great resources:

- *Wild Fermentation* – Sandor Katz
- *The Art of Fermentation* – Sandor Katz
- *Real Food Fermentation* – Alex Lewin
- *Fermented* – Jill Ciciarelli
- *Nourishing Traditions* – Sally Fallon
- *The Permaculture Book of Ferment and Human Nutrition* – Bill Mollison

See page 176 for a recipe for kimchi; page 174 for red cabbage, beetroot and currant sauerkraut; page 178 for white cabbage and celery sauerkraut; page 183 for bee mead; page 182 for fermented lemonade; page 180 for kombucha; and page 179 for pear vinegar.

SMOKING

Smoking involves the infusion of smoke and, in the case of hot smoking, heat, to flavour and preserve food. There are few limits on what you can smoke, and although traditionally used in the preparation of fish, smoking works brilliantly with game, poultry, cheese, vegetables, fruit, nuts and even beer. Smoking is performed either hot or cold. Cold smoking uses no heat, or very low heat, for up to 24 hours. Hot smoking preserves by drying out the food, so there is less moisture for bacteria to grow in, while the heat kills microbes, and chemicals in the smoke actively preserve the food.

Over the years, we've experimented with both cold smoking and hot smoking. Typically, we use cold smoking purely as a flavour introduction to foods

like dairy that don't need to be cooked or that you intend on cooking later. We became interested in hot smoking, on the other hand, because of its intense flavour and preserving qualities. For example, if you hot smoke a fish, it will keep for a good 6 weeks in the fridge, compared to 4–5 days if raw, and if you store the fish in cryovac bags, you will get months out of them. Hot smoking is also a nutritious way of cooking because it doesn't require oil or fat. We've had a couple of fails by applying too much heat, and simply cooking the produce without actually smoking it. Smoking is basically about perfecting the skill of slow cooking.

See page 171 for a recipe for easy smoked salmon; page 172 for smoked sardines, mackerel, oysters and potatoes; page 167 for tea-smoked salt; and page 162 for smoky orange and passionfruit marmalade.

PICKLING

Pickling involves preserving foods by anaerobic fermentation in either an acid, like vinegar, or in brine.

The biggest variables when pickling include ambient temperature, the size of the produce being pickled and the strength of the brine. You can find many great books about pickling that will guide you through these variables, but here is a simple recipe for brined pickles that can be applied to just about any produce:

10 small pickling cucumbers (the fresher the cucumber, the crunchier the pickle), scrubbed
2 garlic cloves, smashed with the back of a knife
2 fresh bay leaves
1 tablespoon mixed pickling spices (cloves, coriander seeds, allspice, pepper and mustard seeds)
1 handful of dill fronds
2 tablespoons salt flakes dissolved in 1½ cups water

Layer a sterilised jar (see page 155 for instructions on sterilising) with the cucumbers, garlic, bay leaves, spices and dill, making sure to leave a good 2.5-cm space between the top of the cucumbers and the

lid of the jar. Fill the jar with the brine and seal with the lid. Give the jar a good shake and place in a cool, dark place. Open the jar every week or so to release the gases produced from the fermentation, and enjoy after 2 weeks.

Texture is so important with pickling, as you don't want your produce to lose its integrity and become mushy. Sandor Katz recommends putting a grape leaf into your pickling crock to keep the pickles crunchy.

The scope for experimentation with pickling is great. Traditional garlic and dill pickled cucumbers are hard to beat, but try watermelon rind, cauliflower, pumpkin and even brussels sprouts for a surprisingly delicious pickling experience.

PRESERVES

Whether it's onion marmalade to slather on cooked meats, or just trusty old strawberry jam, preserves are a fantastic way of using up surplus fruit, vegetables and herbs. Traditionally, the need for preserves came after a bountiful harvest when there was an abundance of produce and a need to extend its life before it perished. Jams, relishes, curds, marmalades and chutneys can be paired with both savoury and sweet dishes.

See page 162 for a recipe for smoky orange and passionfruit marmalade; page 161 for tomato relish; and page 163 for lime chutney.

Smoky orange and passionfruit
marmalade (page 162)

Rich tomato relish

Lime and ginger chutney
(page 163)

RICH TOMATO RELISH

I first learnt how to make this relish when I was an apprentice working with a wonderful chef named Klaus Huber. He was extremely patient with the young cocky Mark of yesteryear, and taught me many things about running a kitchen that I still apply today. He's also an incredible fisherman, and I believe the patience he picked up catching elusive blackfish was tested more than once schooling the ratbag 18-year-old apprentice that I was. I believe Klaus used this recipe to hone my knife skills. There is a lot of knife work but it's very low risk, as the effort I spent perfectly chopping onions, garlic and herbs went into the simmering pot only to disintegrate over time to become a rich tomato relish. We still use this recipe today at the Ducks on the steak sandwich, which has been on the menu since day one.

400 ml white vinegar
250 g brown sugar
½ head of celery
1 white onion
5 spring onions
4–5 large garlic cloves
5-cm piece of ginger
3 small red chillies
1 kg tomatoes
½ eggplant
2 corn cobs, kernels sliced off the cob
1½ apples, cored
200 g trimmed pineapple
1 large handful of coriander
1 small handful of lemon thyme, leaves picked
1 large handful of basil, leaves picked
1 large handful of flat-leaf parsley, leaves picked
160 g sundried tomatoes
250 g tomato paste
400 g can diced tomatoes
salt flakes and freshly ground pepper

For this recipe, you will need enough sterilised jars for about 2 kg of relish (see page 155 for instructions on sterilising).

Bring the vinegar and the sugar to the boil in a large saucepan.

While the vinegar comes to the boil, start to chop all the ingredients reasonably finely (don't be too pedantic), adding them to the pan as they're ready – there is no critical order here, but I would start with the aromatics and work my way through the tomatoes, eggplant, corn and fruit and then add the herbs, including the coriander roots and stalks and the sundried tomatoes and tomato paste. Keep the can of tomatoes aside until the end, as this is what we will use to thicken the relish. Simmer for about 2 hours, making sure everything starts to really break down. Add the tomatoes and cook until it has the consistency of a thick relish. Season the relish to taste.

If you want to jar the relish for later use, bring it to just below the boil (be careful, as it's like molten lava) and fill the sterilised jars. Screw on the lids quickly and turn upside down for 30 seconds. Clean the outside of the jars and then cool in the fridge, the lid should suck down pretty hard and make a pop sound when you open it. The relish will keep unopened in the refrigerator for 6 months, and for 1 month once opened.

If you don't need to store the relish for an extended period, cool in a container on a cooling rack on the bench and then refrigerate. This will still keep for a good month. You could also simply halve this recipe, or it can be frozen.

Makes about 2 kg

SMOKY ORANGE AND PASSIONFRUIT MARMALADE

Making marmalade at home is an absolute joy. Not only will it make your kitchen smell amazing, once you've got the knack, you'll never have to resort to the store-bought stuff again. You'll be making little jars for friends in no time. Try incorporating other spices instead of vanilla. Often we have spices sitting around in our cupboards doing nothing, so get amongst them. Try adding some roasted fennel seeds, a little chilli or some bay leaves. Don't be put off by the smoked sugar in this recipe, if you don't want to make your own, you can add a few drops of smoked essence, or just use raw sugar instead.

**1.2 kg oranges, halved, deseeded and thinly sliced
4 passionfruit, pulp removed
700 g raw sugar
1 vanilla pod, split lengthways, seeds scraped**

**Smoked sugar
1 handful of rice, sugar, tea or smoking chips
200 g raw sugar**

For this recipe, you will need enough small sterilised jars to fit about 1 litre of marmalade (see page 155 for instructions on sterilising).

To smoke the sugar, line the base of a large, heavy-based saucepan with foil. Place a handful of rice (or alternative) on the foil and turn the heat to high until it starts to smoke. Once smoking, add the sugar to a metal bowl and place it inside the pan. Make sure that the smoke can circulate around the bowl. Turn off the heat and place a lid on the pan. Stand until cool.

To make the marmalade, add all the ingredients, including the smoked sugar, to a large, heavy-based saucepan with 2 litres of water. Bring to the boil and then turn the heat down to medium. Cook for 1½–2 hours, stirring occasionally to mix in the sugar and to prevent it from catching.

To test the consistency of the marmalade, place a little marmalade on a cold plate and let it cool. This will indicate how thick it'll be once set. When you're happy with the consistency, set aside to cool and thicken a little in the pot before ladling into sterilised jars. Seal with the lids and store in a cool place for up to 6 months. The marmalade needs to be refrigerated once opened.

Makes 1.2 litres

LIME AND GINGER CHUTNEY

My Nana Barney used to make epic fish, chicken and lamb curries that were so spicy they would strip your taste buds. As I got older, I started to appreciate the complex flavours of those curries. One condiment that was always on the table was lime chutney. Good lime chutney adds an incredible salty, bitter and spicy overlay to the curry base. I consider condiments on a curry night to be just as important as the curry itself.

1 kg limes, roughly chopped into 1.5–2-cm chunks, skin on
2 tablespoons salt flakes
1 teaspoon green cardamom seeds
2 teaspoons coriander seeds
2 heaped teaspoons cumin seeds
1 teaspoon yellow mustard seeds
1 cinnamon stick, crushed
1 heaped teaspoon black peppercorns
3 tablespoons chilli flakes
4 tablespoons vegetable oil
3 garlic cloves, finely grated
75 g fresh ginger, finely grated
1 bunch of fresh coriander, roots only, finely chopped
700 g palm sugar
150 ml fish sauce

For this recipe, you will need enough sterilised jars for about 1.5 kg of chutney (see page 155 for instructions on sterilising).

Add the chopped lime and salt to a medium stainless steel bowl and mix well. Set aside for an hour. Toss the mix and drain, but don't wash the salt off.

In a large, heavy-based frying pan, toast the cardamom, coriander, cumin and mustard seeds with the cinnamon and peppercorns over medium heat. Make sure to continuously stir or shake the spices so they don't burn. Once the spices are fragrant and have coloured slightly, blitz them coarsely in a spice grinder with the chilli flakes.

Add the spices back to the pan with the oil, garlic, ginger and coriander roots and cook, stirring constantly, until the ginger softens. Add the sugar and cook for 5 minutes on high heat. Add the fish sauce. As you see a spicy caramel form, add the limes. When the liquid comes to the boil, cook for a further 3 minutes and then turn off the heat. It's important not to cook the limes for too long, as the mixture will develop a very bitter flavour. However, if this does happen, the bitterness will pass over time in the jar.

While the mix is still very hot, carefully spoon into sterilised glass jars and immediately seal with the lids. Turn the jars upside down for a minute to sterilise the top of the jar and lid. You know you've done a good job when the lid sucks down and a vacuum forms. Store in a cool place for up to 6 months. Once open, store in the fridge for up to 6 weeks. If you plan to use the pickle immediately, you can simply cool in a container on a cooling rack before refrigerating – this will still last for around 6 weeks. Stand for a week or two for any bitterness to dissipate before using.

Makes about 1.5 kg

SPICY KIMCHI CHIPS

When I was a kid I despised brussels sprouts. My poor mum would try anything to get my sister and me to eat all our veggies. Now I can't get enough of them, cooked in nut-brown butter with a little garlic and lemon juice, or shaved over salads to add crunch and flavour. This is an easy little snack. You will need a dehydrator, which you can pick up online — they're not very expensive and have loads of uses. Dehydrating veggies is a great way to get your kids to eat them. These kimchi chips are a spicy little snack for grown-ups, but if you're cooking for the younger ones, just omit the chilli as these do have a nice bit of kick.

12 large brussels sprouts
 (about 400 g)
2 teaspoons salt flakes
1 garlic clove, finely grated
2-cm piece of ginger,
 finely grated
2 teaspoons gochugaru
 (Korean chilli powder)
1½ tablespoons fish sauce
1½ tablespoons soy sauce

Trim the base of each sprout so that the whole leaves peel away easily. Keep trimming the core as you peel to remove all the leaves intact. Place the leaves in a large bowl, add the salt, toss, and set aside for 30 minutes.

Rinse the salt from the sprout leaves and dry using paper towel or a salad spinner.

Mix the garlic, ginger, chilli powder, fish sauce and soy sauce in a large bowl. Add the sprout leaves and toss to evenly coat. Set aside to marinate for 2 hours.

Place the leaves in the dehydrator on medium for about 12 hours to dry completely. Once dry, store the chips in an airtight container or glass jar for up to 3 months.

Serves 2

ZINGY PINEAPPLE, MANGO AND LIME SHERBET

This little number combines two of my favourite things: mango and sherbet. I was a big fan of sherbet as a kid, and when I came to Australia I was completely blown away after tasting my first mango. Nothing like the sour rocks we would get in the UK. The beauty of this recipe is that there is no added sugar. It just uses the natural sugar of the fruit, so it's a lot better for you than conventional sherbet. Also, it's a lot more fun making your own!

200 g dried mango (with no added sugar), finely chopped
400 g peeled pineapple, cut into medium chunks
finely grated zest of ½ lime
½ teaspoon bicarbonate of soda
1 teaspoon citric acid

Using a food processor, blend the mango, pineapple and lime zest to a smooth puree.

Spread the puree about 3-mm thick on dehydrator trays and dry on medium. After 5–6 hours you will have delicious fruit leather, which makes a great little snack, or keep drying for another 20 hours until completely dehydrated to make the sherbet.

Using a mortar and pestle, crush the dried fruit to a powder. Add the bicarbonate of soda and citric acid and combine. You now have naturally sweet pineapple, mango and lime sherbet. This is great on chocolate desserts, mixed with salt to rim glasses for cocktails, or used as a fruit dip as a treat for the kids. Store in an airtight container for up to 3 months.

Makes ¾ cup

CAVOLO NERO CRISPS

Sometimes I get a bit too excited at the farmers' market and buy more produce than I can use. Besides freezing soups and making kraut or pickles, another really handy way of preserving leafy greens is to dry them. Drying allows you to store them for a lot longer and it also concentrates the flavour. You can use them as crackers for cheese or dips, as a vessel for canapés, or to put through salads to give them a bit of texture. It's worth using the larger leaves for this as they do shrink a lot when dehydrated.

2 handfuls of cavolo nero, leaves stripped from woody stems but left on the finer ones
2 tablespoons olive oil
juice of ½ lemon
1 pinch of salt flakes

Wash the cavolo nero in cold water and dry in a salad spinner.

Place the leaves in a large bowl, add the olive oil, lemon juice and salt and toss – also try experimenting with flavoured salts (see page 22), using them before and after drying. Arrange the leaves on the dehydrator trays so that they're not touching each other, and dry on a medium setting for about 12 hours until crisp. Store in an airtight container for up to 3 months.

Serves 2

TEA-SMOKED SALT

Despite sounding quite fancy, tea-smoked salt is actually very easy to make. The trick is to set up an apparatus so the salt doesn't mix with the smoking tea. This is where it's important to have the largest flake salt you can get your hands on – don't try this with regular table salt. You're going to make smoke, and lots of it, so make sure your exhaust fan is on, and the kitchen window is open. If you want to make this a little more interesting, finely chop some fresh rosemary and add it to the salt before smoking – you'll end up with a tea-smoked, rosemary salt that is especially delicious with lamb dishes.

3 tablespoons loose-leaf black tea
250 g large salt flakes

Line the base of a medium, heavy-based saucepan with foil. Add the tea and place over high heat. Add the salt to a fine sieve and fit it over the pan. Once the tea has really started to smoke, place the lid over the sieve – it won't seal properly but that doesn't matter – turn off the heat and smoke for a good 5 minutes. Store the salt in a dry glass jar until needed.

Makes 250 g

BEEF JERKY WITH SMOKED PAPRIKA AND LIME

I'm a big fan of jerky, it's a great snack for road trips, which, I guess, is why it's often found at fuel stops. I still prefer to make my own, though. It's super easy with loads of variations. You can play around with different spice combos, change up the citrus, and use an endless variety of chilli to make those hours on the road a little more exciting. I'm using flank for this recipe, but it works well with lots of other lean red meat cuts. You can use seafood too: salmon and trout both work a treat.

500 g flank steak, fat trimmed
3 tablespoons soy sauce
2 tablespoons Worcestershire sauce
1 tablespoon honey
finely grated zest and juice of ½ lime
1 garlic clove, finely grated
½ teaspoon finely grated ginger
1 teaspoon smoked paprika
1 teaspoon freshly ground black pepper

It's easier to slice the meat when it's really cold, so place it in the freezer for 40 minutes before cutting. Slice the meat across the grain into 2–3-mm thick strips.

Combine the other ingredients in a large bowl. Add the sliced steak and mix to thoroughly coat, cover and refrigerate for 2 hours. Remove from the refrigerator and drain any liquid off in a colander.

Arrange the beef strips on the dehydrator trays, ensuring that they're not touching each other, and dry on medium for about 12 hours.

Once dried to your liking, store in an airtight container in the refrigerator.

Makes about 250 g

EASY SMOKED SALMON

Well, the name says it all. This is a very easy hot-smoking method that can be used on any oily fish, such as salmon, bonito, sardines or kingfish. Hot smoking helps to get a bit more shelf life out of your fish, but I doubt you'll want to hang on to it after you taste how good it is. Perfect for breakfast with poached eggs, wrap it in a cloth and take it to a picnic with a bit of sourdough, or serve straight from the oven for a hot smoky flavour at dinner time.

2 cups hickory woodchips (or use apple bark or whatever else you like)
1 side of salmon (1.2–1.6 kg), skin on, scaled and pin-boned
1 tablespoon brown sugar
2 tablespoons salt flakes
1 small handful of dill, finely chopped
finely grated zest of ½ lemon
freshly ground pepper

For this recipe, you'll need to make an improvised smoker using a deep-sided tray large enough to fit the salmon, a wire cooling rack that will fit inside this tray and a large tray to form a lid.

Preheat the oven to 185°C fan-forced (205°C conventional). Line the deep tray with foil and sprinkle the woodchips over the top. Fit the cooling rack into the tray.

Rub the flesh of the salmon with the sugar, sprinkle over the salt, dill and lemon zest and grind over plenty of pepper. Place the salmon, skin-side down, on the rack and place the tray over medium heat on the stovetop. This is a dry heat method: the flame will heat through the tray and foil causing the woodchips to smoke. When a good amount of smoke is being generated, cover with the large tray to create a little smokehouse. Smoke the fish for 3–5 minutes – you want to see some dark caramel tones forming on the fish and for it have turned more orange.

Take the smoker off the heat and remove the tray that is forming the lid. Line this tray with baking paper. Carefully lift the salmon off the rack and onto the tray. Place in the oven for 14 minutes and then set aside somewhere warm for 10–15 minutes.

Serve immediately or chill to use later.

Serves 6–8

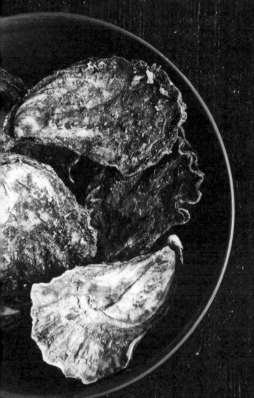

GET SMOKING!

These recipes all use the same simple technique as the easy smoked salmon (see page 171). The only difference is that they don't all require baking after smoking as in the salmon recipe. Once you've mastered the technique, you can get experimental and try smoking all kinds of things!

Mackerel

1 tablespoon brown sugar
1 large handful of dill, fronds picked and
    roughly chopped
1 teaspoon mustard seeds, blanched
finely grated zest of 1 lemon
4 mackerel fillets
salt flakes and freshly ground pepper

Combine the sugar, dill, mustard seeds and lemon zest in a small bowl and rub evenly over the mackerel fillets. Season heavily and place in the smoker for 6–8 minutes.

Rest for 10 minutes before serving. Serve the mackerel hot or cold.

Serves 4–6

Oysters

24 live oysters
lemon wedges, to serve

Shuck the oysters (see page 110), drain off the liquid and place the whole shells in the smoker for 3–5 minutes.

Serve with a good squeeze of lemon.

Serves 4–6

Sardines

finely grated zest of 1 lemon
1 large handful of flat-leaf parsley, leaves picked
    and roughly chopped
1 tablespoon chilli flakes
1 tablespoon salt flakes
20 whole sardines
freshly ground pepper

Combine the lemon zest, parsley, chilli and salt in a
small bowl. Sprinkle the mix over the sardines, grind
over some pepper and smoke for 3–5 minutes.

Serve the sardines hot or cold.

Serves 4–6

Potatoes

600 g chat potatoes, skin on
5 sprigs of rosemary, leaves picked and
    finely chopped
5 sprigs of thyme, leaves picked and finely chopped
1 tablespoon salt flakes
freshly ground pepper
2 tablespoons vegetable oil

Preheat the oven to 200°C fan-forced
(220°C conventional).

Boil the potatoes until soft, drain and cut in half
lengthways.

Sprinkle the potatoes with the rosemary, thyme and
salt. Grind over some pepper and smoke for 5 minutes.

Place on a baking tray and bake for 15 minutes until
they crisp up.

Serves 4

RIDICULOUSLY GOOD RED SAUERKRAUT

Sauerkraut is an unreal probiotic and a brilliant accompaniment to almost any dish: breakfast with poached eggs; with a piece of grilled fish; or you can even add it to salads. There's a touch of the mad scientist about this one. Fizzing and bubbling vegetables mightn't be what we're used to, but I can assure you, the results are yummy and your body will love its new addition of gut flora. Have a play around with different vegetables and different fermenting periods, the longer you leave it on the bench the more intense the ferment flavour will be. You should also gift out a jar, you never know what may come back your way.

½ **red cabbage**
3 **beetroots, trimmed and peeled**
1 **red onion, finely sliced**
250 g **currants**
1 **teaspoon coarsely ground pepper**
salt flakes

For this recipe, you will need four sterilised 1-litre glass jars with airtight lids (see page 155 for instructions on sterilising).

Shred the cabbage on a mandoline set at about 2 mm. Insert the julienne cutter and cut the beetroot the same thickness – you could also shred the cabbage with a knife and coarsely grate the beetroot. Tare your scales with a large bowl. Add the cabbage, beetroot, onion, currants and pepper to the bowl and weigh the contents. It should weigh around 1.5–2 kg.

Weigh out the salt to 5 per cent of the weight of the vegetables. So, for every 100 g of vegetables you will need 5 g of salt. For instance, if the mix weighs 2 kg you will need 100 g of salt.

Sprinkle the salt evenly over the cabbage and beetroot mix and start to work with your hands. It's very important to not use gloves during this process, as we need bacteria from your hands to start the ferment. Massage the salt into the vegetables for a good 5–6 minutes, you will start to see the cabbage becoming soft and almost a bit translucent and there will also be a lot more liquid in the bowl as the salt leaches juice from the vegetables.

Pack the mix into the jars, leaving about 5-cm headspace. This should be packed moderately firmly, don't jam it in too tightly but make sure there are no air pockets. Distribute any remaining liquid evenly across the jars. Push the vegetables under the liquid so that they are fully submerged. Seal the jars and leave on the bench to ferment.

During the fermenting process, open the lids over a sink every 24 hours to release any gas. Also, taste it every time you open it, the flavours will develop over time. I like to ferment mine for only around 3–4 days, but it's up to you. Once you're happy with the flavour, refrigerate to slow down the process. The sauerkraut can be stored for 6 months in the fridge unopened, and for 2 months once opened.

There should be a light fizzing sound as you open the jars, this is nothing to worry about, but if you see any signs of colourful mould, discard the whole batch and start again. Mould will typically form if the vegetables are not totally submerged in the liquid.

Makes 4 × 1-litre jars

THREE BLUE DUCKS' KIMCHI

Don't be afraid of making your own kimchi – you'll be amazed at how easy it is, and so, so tasty. One of my go-to dishes in Sydney is a big bowl of ramen with a side of kimchi and a boiled egg. I crave the stuff. We sometimes serve it at the Ducks with braised ox tongue, but at home it's great with a simple fried egg on toast, or with some steamed vegetables and fried rice.

100 g coarse sea salt
1 small Chinese cabbage
100 g rice flour
5 garlic cloves, finely grated
4-cm piece of ginger, finely grated
8 red radishes, finely sliced
5 spring onions, white and green parts, cut into 1-cm lengths
3 tablespoons soy sauce
3 tablespoons fish sauce
100 g gochugaru (Korean chilli powder)

For this recipe, you will need two 750 ml sterilised glass jars (see page 155 for instructions on sterilising).

In a large glass or plastic container, dissolve the salt in 2 litres of cold water. Cut the cabbage in half lengthways, slice into 3-cm wide pieces and add to the brine. Refrigerate for 12 hours.

Bring 800 ml of water to the boil and whisk in the rice flour. Cook while stirring until the mix resembles wallpaper paste. Take off the heat and transfer to a large bowl to cool slightly.

Add the garlic, ginger, radish, spring onion, soy, fish sauce and chilli powder to the paste and combine. Remove the cabbage from the brine, squeezing out any excess liquid, and add to the bowl. Give the mix a good stir, check the seasoning and chilli level and adjust to taste. Transfer to the sterilised jar. Make sure the cabbage is packed in tightly and that all the mix is submerged in liquid. Place the lid on the jar and leave at room temperature for 24 hours to ferment.

After 24 hours, carefully open the lids to release any gas – do this over the sink, as it can be a bit messy. Taste the kimchi to see how the fermentation is progressing. Repeat this process over a couple of days until you are happy with the sourness of the kimchi. When satisfied with the fermented character, store in the refrigerator for up to 6 months unopened, and for 2 months once opened.

Makes 2 × 750 ml jars

WHITE CABBAGE AND CELERY SAUERKRAUT

Since our introduction to the world of fermentation (thanks to Sandor Katz), I often experiment with various kraut recipes, as kraut is where the obsession begins. I've tried incorporating different spices: cinnamon, coriander seeds, cloves, bay leaves, wattle and juniper, and all with varying degrees of success. I quickly learnt not to be too heavy-handed with flavouring as the fermenting process seems to extract so much flavour from the spices that they can quickly overpower the kraut. Also, adding other vegetables such as carrot, beetroot or a little kale, works well. So far my favourite combo is this recipe, simply white cabbage and celery.

1 teaspoon coriander seeds (optional)
1 teaspoon fennel seeds (optional)
1 large (about 2 kg) white cabbage, dark leaves removed
3 celery stalks, cut into 3-mm slices
2 tablespoons salt

You will need two sterilised 900 ml jars for this recipe (see page 155 for instructions on sterilising).

Toast the coriander and fennel seeds (if using) in a dry frying pan until fragrant and lightly coloured.

Peel off two of the outer leaves of the cabbage and reserve. Cut the cabbage into quarters, remove the core and shred the leaves about 3-mm thick.

Add the shredded cabbage, celery and salt to a large bowl and, using your hands, mix for about 2 minutes – the trick here is to mix it quite vigorously, so that the salt can break down the cells of the vegetables. Set aside for 10 minutes.

The mix should now be quite wet. Give it another mix for a couple of minutes and it's ready to jar. Add the coriander and fennel seeds (you can use any spices you like here, cumin or mustard seeds would also work well, but 2 teaspoons is enough) and mix through. Taste the liquid and if it's a little bland, add a little more salt; if it's too salty, just add a little water.

Take one of the jars and stuff the cabbage in. You can be reasonably firm at this stage; as you push it in you'll notice more liquid being released. Fill it all the way to the top, ensuring that the liquid covers the cabbage and there are no air pockets. Take one of the reserved, unsalted leaves, fold it up and place it on top – this will hold down the kraut when you close the lid. Repeat the process with the second jar. Store the sauerkraut on a tray somewhere cool and away from sunlight to ferment.

During the fermenting process, open the lids over a sink every 24 hours to release any gas. Once you're happy with the strength of the kraut (and this really is a matter of personal preference), which can take 2–7 days, store in the refrigerator. The kraut will keep for up to 6 months unopened, and for 2 months once opened.

Makes 2 × 900 ml jars

FERMENTED PEAR VINEGAR

After seeing the inspirational Sandor Katz speak about the art of fermentation, we were really encouraged to take a curious and experimental approach to this technique. Some things that we might have previously thrown away now looked like exciting new opportunities. We'd been using these red sensation sweet pears from a mate with an organic farm (part of the reason for a great result, I'm sure). We had a whole heap that were on the way to turning, and Darren came up with the idea of giving vinegar-making a go. So we did.

The first thing he did was blitz the pears and pass them through some coffee filter papers. He added the liquid to a stainless steel bowl with a wide rim, covered it with a cloth and then kept it in a warm dark environment (above the ice machine motor) to let the natural bacteria of our world do their thing.

We were flying to Paris a week later, so we didn't have the opportunity to watch the development take place, but when we came home a month later, there was something truly special waiting for us. Direct quote from Daz: 'Best f#cking vinegar I have ever tasted.' And that's good enough for me.

This same technique will work with sweet apples as well, and, needless to say, there isn't really a recipe. I would recommend using a minimum of ten pieces of fruit so that there's something left at the end of your experiment. To help things along, stir the liquid every day for the first ten days.

The time this process will take is quite variable, if the fruit is really overripe, chances are it's already fermenting and everything should be well on track. As the sugars are converted to alcohol, that alcohol can then be converted to vinegar. A moderately warm place will help this process; if it's too cold the yeasts will shut down. The best guide is to simply smell and taste every now and then, and have a little patience. If at any stage a colourful fungus forms on the surface of the liquid, discard the whole batch and start again. Once you're happy with the flavour, store the vinegar in a sealed jar in the fridge for up to 6 months.

HAN'S CHIA PUDDING WITH COCONUT AND YOGHURT

This was a dish that my girlfriend Hannah made when we were living in Bondi. It was at the start of our health food journey and we had an excessive amount of chia seeds. Hannah had noticed that when you add liquid to chia seeds they become swollen and jelly-like, very similar to cooked tapioca. We thought that we could make a raw porridge, so we conducted a little experiment that turned out quite well. This is something that you prepare the night before and it will last for two days.

125 g chia seeds
1 young coconut, water
   removed and flesh chopped
200 g mixed frozen berries
150 g yoghurt, plus extra
your favourite nuts and
   seeds, to serve
raw honey or honeycomb,
   to serve
fresh berries, to serve

For this recipe, you will need a 1-litre glass jar with a lid.

Add the chia seeds, coconut water and flesh, and berries to the jar and mix. It will be quite a grainy and gooey mix to start with, but don't worry, the chia seeds will draw a lot of moisture out of the berries and it will thicken and become more gelatinous. Put on the lid and refrigerate overnight.

In the morning, stir the yoghurt through the mix. If it's a bit dry or a bit too gooey, stir through a little more yoghurt until you reach your desired consistency.

Serve in breakfast bowls with some sesame seeds, roasted almonds, hazelnuts, pumpkin seeds or any other seeds and nuts that you like. Drizzle over some honey (or add some honeycomb), scatter over a couple of berries and serve.

Serves 4

HONEY, YOGHURT AND GOAT'S CHEESE SEMIFREDDO

This is ideal if you want a frozen dessert but don't have an ice cream machine. It may seem like a lot of whisking, but it's actually an incredibly easy dessert that takes minutes to prepare. If figs aren't in season, strawberries are also great with honey and goat's cheese.

70 g buckwheat kernels
3 eggs, separated
1 tablespoon honey,
   plus extra
250 ml Greek yoghurt
150 g soft goat's cheese
salt flakes
250 ml cream
1 vanilla pod, split
   lengthways, seeds scraped
1 tablespoon caster sugar
60 g roasted hazelnuts, peeled
4 figs

Preheat the oven to 180°C fan-forced (200°C conventional). Line a 30-cm loaf tin with plastic wrap and place in the freezer.

Spread the buckwheat out on a baking tray and roast until golden, about 4 minutes. Set aside to cool.

Add the egg yolks to a large bowl and whisk until pale. Whisk in the honey, yoghurt, goat's cheese and a pinch of salt until smooth.

In a medium bowl, whisk the cream and vanilla seeds until soft peaks form.

In another medium bowl, whisk the eggwhites and sugar until stiff. It's really important that the bowl and whisk or beaters are clean and dry, otherwise the eggwhites won't become stiff and form peaks.

Using a spatula, fold the cream mix into the yolk mix until combined. Fold in the eggwhite mix and follow with the hazelnuts and buckwheat (reserving some buckwheat for garnish). Pour into the prepared tin and freeze overnight.

When ready to serve, scoop the semifreddo into bowls. Serve with torn figs, a drizzle of honey and the reserved buckwheat scattered over top.

Serves 8

SWEETS
& DRINKS

MISO-CARAMEL BAKED APPLES

This is a fabulous recipe for a cold winter's night. The salt from the miso is great with the caramel, add all the spices with the baked fruit and you've got yourself a winner. Have a go at using pears or peaches, just adjust the cooking time – the firmer the fruit, the longer it needs. I've also tried this a couple of times on an open wood barbecue. Just place the foil-wrapped apples in the embers and watch the butter, sugar and juices bubble away. Serve with ice cream or double cream.

2 tablespoons unsalted butter
6 golden delicious or granny smith apples, cored

Stuffing
4 tablespoons slivered almonds
1 tablespoon pumpkin seeds
2 tablespoons rolled oats
3 tablespoons dark brown sugar
1 tablespoon white miso paste
1 teaspoon mixed spice
4 tablespoons raisins
2 teaspoons chia seeds
finely grated zest and juice of 1 orange

Preheat the oven to 180°C fan-forced (200°C conventional).

For the stuffing, toast the almonds, pumpkin seeds and oats in separate batches in a dry frying pan until slightly golden.

Tear off six squares of foil large enough to wrap the apples with, and grease each with the butter. Wrap the apples in the foil, leaving the top exposed to take the stuffing, and place on a baking tray.

Combine all the stuffing ingredients in a medium bowl and fill the apples, pressing any leftover stuffing on top of the apples. Bake for 15–20 minutes until tender and caramelised. Serve in the middle of the table still wrapped in foil, or unwrap and plate the apples individually, with some vanilla ice cream or double cream on the side.

Serves 6

RHUBARB, ORANGE AND ROSEMARY CAKE

Like many, my first taste of rhubarb was in Mum's crumble. I used to love the stuff, with good old custard from a tin. It's amazing gently poached in a little spiced sugar syrup and served with rice pudding, or even in savoury dishes, such as roasted duck with some honey and bitter leaves. For this recipe, we've gone back to dessert. Orange, rhubarb and rosemary work brilliantly. But of course you could try it with strawberries and lemon thyme, cherries and chocolate, or figs and licorice.

120 g unsalted butter, softened

160 g raw sugar, plus 3 teaspoons extra

2 eggs, lightly beaten with a fork

50 g almond meal

finely grated zest of ½ small orange and juice of 1 small orange

100 g plain flour

1 teaspoon baking powder

1 pinch of salt flakes

250 g rhubarb, peeled and cut into 2-cm pieces

1 rosemary sprig

crème fraîche, to serve

Preheat the oven to 180°C fan-forced (200°C conventional). Grease a rectangular cake tin and line with baking paper.

Whisk the butter and 160 g of sugar in a large bowl until pale and smooth. Slowly add the eggs, adding a tablespoon of the almond meal just before the last bit of egg – this will stabilise the mix and stop it from splitting when the juice is added – and then mix in the orange zest and juice.

In another bowl, combine the flour, baking powder, salt and remaining almond meal. Fold the dry ingredients into the butter mix and then spoon the mix into the prepared tin. Arrange the rhubarb on top of the cake. Break the rosemary into 6–7 pieces and spike into the mix. Sprinkle 3 teaspoons of sugar on top of the cake and bake for about 50 minutes. It's ready when a skewer comes out clean. Set aside to cool.

Once cooled, serve the cake with crème fraîche.

Serves 6

THE COLOMBIAN EXPRESS

This dish first featured at the Ducks three years ago, when we had a beautiful Colombian girl named Laura working for us. She brought an amazing energy to the kitchen; she was cheeky, funny and very talented. This is a take on a dish that she put on the menu when she was working the dessert section. There are a few stages to make this – the chargrilled pineapple, dulce de leche, chilli granita and yoghurt jelly – but they're all easy and when you put them together you get a well-balanced textural dessert that is delicious, and will leave your friends and family thinking you're a superstar! You will need to prepare this the night before.

395 g can sweetened
   condensed milk
¼ fresh pineapple, cut into
   8-mm thick slices
1 handful of heavily roasted
   cashews, roughly chopped
1 handful of red-veined sorrel
   leaves (optional)

Yoghurt jelly
1 leaf gold-strength gelatine
70 g sugar
165 g natural yoghurt

Chilli granita
2 long red chillies, roughly
   chopped
½ bunch of coriander,
   roots only
100 g palm sugar
50 ml ginger juice
finely grated zest and juice
   of 2 limes

First, make the yoghurt jelly. Soak the gelatine in cold water for 5 minutes. Meanwhile, place the sugar in a small saucepan with 70 ml of water. Bring to the boil to dissolve the sugar, then remove from the heat and leave to cool. Lift the gelatine out of the water and squeeze out any excess water with your hands. Add to the sugar syrup and stir to dissolve. Add the yoghurt to a medium bowl and then whisk in the syrup. Pour into a small container and set in the fridge overnight.

To make the granita, add the chillies, coriander roots and 300 ml of water to a small saucepan and simmer for 2 minutes. Add the palm sugar and stir until dissolved. Set aside for an hour or so to infuse.

Once infused, strain and stir in the ginger juice, lime zest and lime juice. Pour into a tray or container – you need enough surface area to scrape up the granita with a fork – and freeze overnight.

To make the dulce de leche, place the unopened tin of condensed milk in boiling water and boil for 3 hours. Carefully remove from the water and set aide to cool for 30 minutes. Very carefully open the tin (the contents will be molten) and set aside.

When you're ready to serve, preheat the barbecue grill on high.

Grill the pineapple until you see some nice black grill marks forming, turn over and repeat on the other side.

To serve, loosely arrange the grilled pineapple on a serving plate. Using a teaspoon, scoop out a generous amount of yoghurt jelly. Using another teaspoon, scrape the jelly off the first spoon and onto the pineapple. Do the same with the dulce de leche and then sprinkle over the cashews. Using a fork, scrape the granita into fluffy piles of ice. Spoon a good 2–3 tablespoons of granita per serve onto the pineapple, arrange the red-veined sorrel leaves (if using) over the top and serve immediately.

Serves 4

SWEET POTATO ICE CREAM

I'm a big fan of using vegetables in desserts. We have loads at the Ducks: chocolate and beetroot brownies, fennel ice cream, parsnip cake, candied celery … This ice cream, like many things, goes really well with chocolate.

250 g sweet potato, peeled and cut into 5-cm dice
160 g caster sugar
8 egg yolks
475 ml milk
475 ml cream
1 vanilla pod, split lengthways, seeds scraped
1 tablespoon liquid glucose

Preheat the oven to 180°C fan-forced (200°C conventional). Line a baking tray with baking paper.

Roast the sweet potato on the prepared tray until quite soft with a little colour, about 30 minutes. Set aside to cool for 5 minutes in a large bowl.

Whisk the sugar and egg yolks in a large bowl until pale and smooth. Add the cooled sweet potato and mix in.

Fill a large bowl with ice and water.

Add the milk, cream, vanilla bean and scraped seeds, and glucose to a medium saucepan over medium heat and bring almost to the boil. Take off the heat and gradually add to the yolk and sweet potato mix while whisking – the sweet potato will break down and incorporate as you whisk. Once amalgamated, return this mix to the pan and gently cook while stirring constantly until it thickens to a consistency that coats the back of a wooden spoon. Strain the mix into a bowl, and chill by placing the bowl in the iced water.

Once cooled, churn in an ice cream machine, then freeze for 1–1½ hours before serving.

Makes about 1 litre

LIME AND COCONUT ICE CREAM

A thoroughly enjoyable ice cream on its own, or better still with sticky rice, roasted peanuts, some mango cheeks and grilled pineapple, or try it with the banana tart on page 213 if you really want to go to town. If you can't get hold of kaffir lime leaves, add the zest of half a lime. When the coconut has done its job flavouring the base, don't throw it out, just add it to a banana smoothie, or give it to the chooks.

475 ml milk
475 ml cream
80 g toasted coconut flakes
3 kaffir lime leaves, bruised
   in your hands
1 tablespoon liquid glucose
180 g caster sugar
8 egg yolks

Place the milk, cream, coconut, lime leaves and glucose in a saucepan, bring almost to the boil and then remove from the heat. Set aside to infuse for 1 hour.

Whisk the sugar and egg yolks in a large bowl until pale and smooth.

Fill a large bowl with ice and water.

Bring the milk and cream mixture back up to just below the boil and immediately strain into a large jug. Gradually pour into the yolk mix while constantly whisking. Once amalgamated, return this mix to the pan and gently cook, stirring constantly, until it thickens to a consistency that coats the back of a spoon. Strain the mix into a bowl, and chill by placing the bowl in the iced water.

Once cooled, churn in an ice cream machine, then freeze for 1–1½ hours before serving.

Makes about 1 litre

NANA BARNEY'S LOVE CAKE

In our family, Nana Barney's love cake is quite possibly the most special thing that you could make for somebody. Dense, moist and full of cashews, with a baked, eggwhite-crusted top — it's just delicious. My brother and I would go to stay with Nan and after dinner she would slice up a piece of love cake, and then, because she had an extreme sweet tooth, she'd slice up a few more. Very few members of our family know how to make Nana Barney's love cake, and she guarded the recipe right up until the time she left us. Just before she died, she passed the recipe on to my stepmother, Carolyn, and for many reasons Carolyn was the best choice, for she has guarded the recipe just as loyally and made it beautifully for us on countless special occasions. Now, there is some controversy as to how I got my hands on this recipe, as well as the fact that I am sharing it with you. But if there was one taste that truly reminds me of my beautiful Grandmother, it's her love cake, and I feel like it's too good a cake to be kept secret. If she were alive today, I think she would giggle with delight at having her recipe in a cookbook. I think she would also have a chuckle at the cheekiness with which I got the recipe.

9 eggs, separated, all 9 yolks but only 5 whites (remaining 4 whites can be frozen for later use)
510 g caster sugar
255 g unsalted butter, melted
2 vanilla pods, split lengthways and seeds scraped
1½ teaspoons finely grated lemon zest
255 g cashews, raw and unsalted, chopped to about the size of the crunchy bits in crunchy peanut butter
255 g medium semolina
1 teaspoon almond essence
double cream, to serve
finely grated lemon zest, to serve

Preheat the oven to 160°C fan forced (180°C conventional). Grease a 20-cm × 30-cm cake tin and line with baking paper.

Beat the eggwhites to stiff peaks and set aside.

Beat the egg yolks with an electric mixer and then gradually add the sugar, half the melted butter, vanilla seeds and lemon zest. Beat the mixture until pale and fluffy. Set aside.

Combine the cashews, semolina, almond essence and remaining melted butter in a medium bowl.

Combine the yolk and the cashew mixtures, and then fold in three-quarters of the beaten eggwhites. Spoon the mixture into the prepared tin, smoothing the top of the surface with the back of a wooden spoon. Evenly cover the top of the cake with the remaining eggwhite. Bake for 1 hour and 10 minutes, checking after 1 hour — the egg whites will start to form a nicely golden crust on top of the cake. Test with a skewer, you want it to come out with a light coating of mix on it. Cool in the tin to firm up before unmoulding.

Serve with double cream and a sprinkling of lemon zest.

Serves 8–10

BANANA TART WITH LEMONGRASS CARAMEL AND CASHEWS

This is basically a banana tarte Tatin. It's an absolute throw together dessert that never fails to impress. Caramelise some sugar, lemongrass and butter on the stove, add some chopped banana, top with a disc of puff pastry, bake for 20 minutes and you're done. If you want to make your own ice cream, great, the lime and coconut ice cream on page 209 is a cracker. Otherwise, a good store-bought vanilla ice cream will more than suffice.

1 puff pastry sheet
80 g raw sugar
2-cm lemongrass stem, white
  part only, bruised
1 tablespoon unsalted butter
1 pinch of salt flakes
4 ripe bananas, peeled and
  cut into 5-cm lengths
1 small handful of roasted
  unsalted cashews, chopped
finely grated zest of ½ lime
8 small mint leaves

Cut a 21–22-cm disc out of the pastry sheet.

Place a heavy 25-cm ovenproof pan over medium–high heat and add the sugar and lemongrass. After a couple of minutes the sugar will begin to melt and turn golden brown. Turn off the heat, add the butter and salt and stir with a wooden spoon until amalgamated. It's really important to take care when making caramel, as the sugar will be scalding hot. Cool the caramel for a minute or so before arranging the banana in a decorative round in the pan – this will be the top of your tart, so take a little care doing it. Top the banana with the puff pastry disc, tucking it around the outside edge of the banana and bake for 25–30 minutes until golden brown. Remove from the oven and rest for 10 minutes.

Once rested, place the pan over medium heat for 30 seconds to loosen the caramel. Place a plate over the tart so that it sits snuggly against the pastry. Using one hand to hold the plate firmly against the tart, and the other to hold the handle of the pan, quickly turn the pan over, place on the benchtop and immediately remove your bottom hand. Carefully lift the pan off the tart. Top with the cashews, lime zest and mint and serve immediately with ice cream.

Serves 4

CHOC-ORANGE BREAD AND BUTTER PUDDING

Growing up, we would occasionally have bread and butter pudding as a treat; Mum would serve it with ice cream after a Sunday roast. It's a lovely dessert for a winter's day, and it never fails to please. It's also a great way to use up stale bread.

80 g butter, at room temperature
finely grated zest of 1 orange
1 vanilla pod, split lengthways, seeds scraped
10 slices sourdough bread
8 eggs
60 g caster sugar
200 g cooking chocolate buttons (70% cocoa)
400 ml cream
400 ml milk
70 g walnuts
50 g sultanas

Preheat the oven to 170°C fan-forced (190°C conventional).

Whip the butter with the orange zest and vanilla seeds.

Grease a deep baking dish with the flavoured butter. Spread the remaining butter on the bread, and cut each slice in half.

In a large bowl, whisk the eggs and sugar until combined, then add half the chocolate.

Add the cream and vanilla pod to a small saucepan and heat to 90°C, or just under the boil. Pour this over the egg and chocolate mix and immediately pour in the milk to cool it down. Stir to amalgamate, and strain.

Layer the prepared tin with the bread, sprinkling walnuts, sultanas and the remaining chocolate between each layer. After completing each layer, pour some of the chocolate mixture over the top and finish by pouring any remaining mixture over the last layer. Set aside for 15 minutes for the bread to soak up the chocolate mixture, and then bake for 25–30 minutes.

The pudding should have a slight wobble once cooked. Serve hot with ice cream.

Serves 8

STRAWBERRY AND FENNEL TARTS

Frangipane is way easier to make than you might think. Get creative with other flavours for this tart: try mixing freshly grated ginger and white chocolate through the frangipane and topping with raspberries. We make our pastry in a food processer, which means you can have it wrapped up and in the fridge within minutes. Don't stress if you haven't got one, though, just go old school. Use your fingertips and work quickly, or the heat from your hands will melt the butter. Adding ingredients to a base pastry recipe is a great way of adding extra texture and flavour. Try using flaxseeds, oats, lime zest, chia seeds or even a little squid ink — whatever takes your fancy.

I teaspoon fennel seeds, toasted
200 g strawberries, hulled and sliced
3 sprigs of lemon thyme, leaves picked
cream or crème fraîche, to serve
I tablespoon fennel flowers (optional)

Mandarin and poppy seed pastry
200 g plain flour, chilled
50 g icing sugar
½ pinch of salt flakes
100 g unsalted butter, diced and chilled
finely grated zest of ½ mandarin
I teaspoon poppy seeds
I egg, whisked

Frangipane
200 g unsalted butter, softened
200 g caster sugar
I vanilla pod, split lengthways, seeds scraped
3 eggs, lightly beaten with a fork
250 g almond meal

To make the pastry by hand, add the flour, sugar and salt to a large bowl and combine. Add the butter and work with your fingertips until it resembles breadcrumbs. Add the mandarin zest and poppy seeds and quickly combine. Add enough of the whisked egg to just bring the mix together (you'll probably only need about half). Gently knead a couple of times until smooth. Flatten out roughly, wrap in plastic wrap and refrigerate for 20 minutes before using.

To make the pastry in a food processor, simply follow the same steps, pulsing until it just reaches each stage without overworking, and then knead and rest as normal.

Preheat the oven to 180°C fan-forced (200°C conventional).

Roll out the pastry on a floured surface until 3–4-mm thick. Cut out circles to line six individual 9-cm tart tins, or one large 25-cm loose-based flan tin. When lining the tins, make sure the pastry is pressed right into the corners. Add a pinch of fennel seeds to the base of each tart and press the seeds into the pastry. Trim the pastry, leaving 4–5-mm overhang to allow for shrinkage, and rest in the fridge for 30 minutes.

Once rested, line the tarts with baking paper and fill with rice or baking weights. Bake for 15 minutes. Remove the paper and rice and cook for another 5 minutes. Set aside to cool before filling.

Turn the oven down to 160°C fan-forced (180°C conventional).

For the frangipane, beat the butter, sugar and vanilla seeds until pale and fluffy, scraping down the sides of the bowl a couple of times as you go. Slowly add the eggs to the mix while beating. Once incorporated, switch off the mixer and fold in the almond meal by hand.

Spoon the frangipane mix into the tart shells, top with the strawberries, remaining fennel seeds and a little lemon thyme. Bake for 15–20 minutes for individual tarts, or 30–35 minutes for a large tart. Once cooked, the frangipane will spring back slightly to the touch. Trim any excess pastry and serve with cream or crème fraîche and fennel flowers if you can find some!

Makes 6 small tarts or I large one

THE PINBONE RICE CUSTARD TART

This recipe is from our friends Mike Eggert and Jemma Whiteman from Pinbone in Sydney. We've known these guys for years — two truly amazing chefs and friends. They've kindly let us use their kick-arse rice custard tart recipe for this book. Probably so that we'll start making it ourselves and finally leave them alone! This recipe is a delicious way to use up any leftover cooked rice in your fridge.

Pastry

250 g plain flour
200 g butter, cut into small dice
100 g icing sugar
1 pinch of salt flakes
2 eggs, separated (you'll use the 2 yolks but only 1 white)

Custard filling

14 egg yolks
600 ml cream
50 g caster sugar
finely grated zest of 1 orange
1 pinch of freshly grated nutmeg
280 g cooked white rice

To make the pastry, blitz the flour, butter, sugar and salt in a food processor until it resembles fine breadcrumbs. Add the yolks and mix until the dough just comes together. Tip onto a floured surface and knead lightly three or four times, form into a ball, wrap in cling film and refrigerate for 1 hour.

After resting, roll out the pastry on a lightly floured surface until it is an even 4-mm thick. Lay over a 26-cm tart shell and line, carefully pushing the pastry into the corners and leaving excess at the rim to allow for shrinkage. Place the lined tin in the fridge for 20–30 minutes to rest.

Preheat the oven to 180°C fan-forced (200°C conventional).

Line the chilled tart shell with baking paper and fill with rice or pastry weights. Bake for 10–15 minutes, rotating halfway through to ensure that it cooks evenly. Carefully remove the baking paper, being sure not to spill the rice or beans into the pastry, and cook for a further 5–7 minutes until the centre of the tart shell is cooked. Brush the shell with the beaten egg white and bake for 2–3 minutes – this helps to seal the pastry from the wet filling. Set the tart shell aside to cool before filling.

Turn the oven down to 130°C fan-forced (150°C conventional).

While the tart shell is cooling, make the custard filling. Beat the yolks and cream together using a wooden spoon (using a whisk will create air bubbles on top of the tart) until combined.

In a separate bowl, combine the sugar, orange zest and nutmeg and then slowly mix in the cream and yolk mixture, again with a spoon, until combined.

Place the tart tin on a baking tray and evenly fill with the rice. Gently pour the custard filling over the top of the rice, and bake in the preheated oven for 30–40 minutes, rotating the tart every 10 minutes to ensure even cooking. The tart is ready when the custard is just set and still slightly wobbly in the centre. Set aside to cool on the bench.

Once cooled to room temperature, trim the pastry if necessary and serve.

Serves 8–10

SPICED PEARS WITH BLUE CHEESE, NUTS AND CRISPBREAD

This is a great cheese course, super-easy to prepare and something that can be done well in advance. The pears will actually take on even more of the spicy flavour if left for a few hours or overnight. A good salty, creamy blue cheese will do the trick. If you're lucky enough to live near a cheese maker, I would recommend making friends with them and using what they have. Otherwise, go for Endeavour Blue, Roquefort or Stilton.

4 corella pears (or
   3 packhams), peeled,
   quartered and cored
blue cheese, to serve
walnuts or roasted hazelnuts,
   to serve
Rustic Crispbread (see page
   73), to serve

Spice syrup
2 cinnamon sticks
4 cloves
2 star anise
250 ml red wine
250 ml orange juice
100 g caster sugar

Place all the spice syrup ingredients in a large saucepan over medium heat and stir until the sugar dissolves. Add the pears and cook for 15–20 minutes on low heat – you don't want to boil the pears or they will be too soft to grill. Stand the pears in the liquid until cool enough to handle.

Remove the pears and the spices from the liquid and return the pan to the heat. Reduce the liquid to a syrup.

Preheat the barbecue grill or a griddle pan on high.

Cook the pears for 1–2 minutes on each side until they start to caramelise and have distinct grill marks.

Serve the pears with a drizzle of the syrup and some blue cheese, nuts and crispbread on the side.

Serves 8

USER'S GUIDE TO

Juicing

Darren used to work with a sous-chef who was convinced that if he drank enough carrot juice he would get a tan. He was a pretty pasty-looking bloke, short, with a strange laugh, but a really good cook. He would drink the stuff every day, and this was before there were juice stores popping up everywhere and before spray tans became all the rage. Today, commercial juice bars peddle their product as the panacea for every problem a person might encounter: a glass of beetroot juice will increase physical performance; a shot of wheatgrass juice will reverse the onset of greying hair; and a daily dose of lemon juice will help you lose weight. All the fads aside, raw juice is a brilliant way to consume far more fruit and vegetables than you normally would.

Most people don't consume enough raw fruits and vegetables. People are overfed and undernourished, which means their digestive systems have been beaten down from years of trying to extract nutrients and dispose of waste from the wrong kind of foods. When you drink raw, unadulterated juice you are drinking a glass of vitamin and mineral-rich fuel that nourishes your body at a cellular level, eliminates waste from your system and fortifies your immunity.

How does it work? Basically, juicing removes the insoluble fibre from fruit and vegetables, allowing for the quick and total absorption of the vitamins, minerals, phytonutrients and antioxidants. Obviously we still need fibre for the colon to function normally. So, juices aren't a substitute for wholefoods, and shouldn't ever replace wholefoods in your diet. A good way of getting around the loss of fibre is to blend some cucumber, kale or spinach into your juice right before serving.

When we first started out as juicers, we favoured sweet and fruity flavours like apple, ginger and lemon, or watermelon, lime and mint. However, the more juice we drank the less sweet we needed it to be. We started using more chlorophyll-rich vegetables like kale, chard and spinach. Then we began playing with all sorts of combinations, adding different fruits and vegetables, but also petals, herbs, roots, weeds and seaweed. These earthy elixirs have become a real daily treat for us.

There are two main juice extraction methods: centrifugal and cold press.

CENTRIFUGAL

Centrifugal juicers shred the fruit and vegetables while spinning them at high speed, which separates the juice from the pulp. Think of the way a washing machine spins off the excess water from your clothes. The advantages of this kind of juicer are that they're commonly available, are cheaper than a cold press, and usually have a wide feeding chute for juicing whole fruits and vegetables which saves time. However, there are some strong arguments against centrifugal juicers: the high speed spinning can cause the produce to oxidise, which destroys enzymes; the high speed blade shredding doesn't penetrate the produce deeply enough to extract all the nutrients; and the extracted juice is primarily water content and separates easily.

COLD PRESS

Cold press juicers masticate the fruit and vegetables, extracting the juice by gently crushing and pressing. The main advantage of this kind of extraction is that it has a slow turning speed and doesn't produce nearly as much heat, so all the vital enzymes, vitamins, and minerals stay intact. A cold press juicer retains up to double the nutrients of a centrifugal juicer.

JUICES

Fresh juice is something that is consumed on a daily basis in our house. Trust me, adding this ritual to your daily routine will most definitely leave you feeling a bit more energised and alert. It's amazing the volume of produce that you can consume with a few simple drinks a day. Keep juices in a glass jar with an airtight lid, but like anything, the longer they hang around, the lower the nutrient value is. And don't buy bottled juice, as most of it has been heat-treated to increase its shelf life – you might as well be drinking a glass of water with food colouring in it, it has about the same nutrient value. My girlfriend Hannah is the juice guru in our house, and she has guided me through these combinations to make sure there is something for everyone.

The method here is pretty simple: juice everything. You can use the pulp you are left with to make crumbs that can be used in a wide range of dishes (see page 27). Alternatively, compost the scraps or put them in a worm farm – the size of the pulp is perfect worm food.

With all these juices, if the flavour is a bit too intense, add some water, if they're not sweet enough, add some apple, orange or watermelon. What you'll find is that over time your taste buds won't crave the sweet so much, but rather the savoury juice of the vegetables.

All juices serve 2

Red

500 g watermelon, rind removed
2 beetroot, peeled but juice the
    stalks and leaves too
4 celery stalks
1 large handful of mint
½ lemon, peeled
1 long red chilli (deseeded if you
    don't like the heat)

Yellow

3 oranges, peeled
1 lemon, peeled
2 carrots
4-cm piece of ginger
4-cm piece of turmeric

Green

⅓ bunch of kale (about 200 g)
1 green apple
1 Lebanese cucumber
½ handful of parsley
1 handful of baby spinach
4-cm piece of ginger
½ lemon, peeled

SMOOTHIES

These smoothies are goodness in a glass. They can be made in advance and consumed over a few days; in some cases, they might not taste so sweet when you make them, but after a day they seem to sweeten up. Always add a couple of ice cubes to the mix to keep the temperature down while blending. This will help to preserve the nutritional value of the produce. Use quality organic produce, and keep it local if you can.

Coconut, strawberry and chia

With all the smoothies, just add the ingredients to a blender and whizz for a minute or so, remembering to add some ice to keep the temperature down.

All smoothies serve 2

1 young coconut, flesh and water
300 ml almond milk
250 g strawberries
1 banana
1 tablespoon chia seeds
1 tablespoon maca powder

Green

1 young coconut, flesh and water
1 avocado, peeled and pitted
1 Lebanese cucumber
1 handful of baby spinach
1 kiwi fruit, peeled
1 banana, peeled
1 tablespoon chia seeds
200 ml almond milk

Banana, mango and chocolate

600 ml almond milk
1 young coconut, flesh and water
1 banana, peeled
½ mango, peeled and stoned
60 g blueberries
2 tablespoons cacao nibs

Thank You!

DARREN

Huge thanks to the family. My partner in crime, Magdalena Roze, for constantly taming the giraffe and for looking out for me. Mum, for always being there and supporting me though the years. My sister Abbie, Jamie, Sam and Tom. Alicia, John, Karolina and Team Poland. The Surf Hell men: Gez, Zen, Jonny NBS Wilson – miss you, me old pal. Amanda Ryan, my oldest friend in Oz. Tracy, Justine and the Chefs Ink crew. To Marky, who makes so much of this happen, it's been a pleasure to work with you on this mate. And to the chickens and bees …

MARK

I would like to say a big thank you to everyone who helped to put together such a lovely book. This has been the most enjoyable experience, an amazing time of reflection on how I became the chef I am today and the incredible people I have met and worked with along the way.

I would like to make special mention of my Nana Barney, who always supported me and loved me unconditionally right up until she passed. It's strange that it has taken so long for me to realise the influence she has had on my food journey, but it's there and when I think of the flavours of my past I always find her resurfacing in my thoughts. So thank you, Nan, wherever you are.

To Hannah, you are the most amazing human I have ever had the pleasure of spending time with. You regularly surprise me with your intelligence and generosity. Thank you for doing such an amazing job with this book. I saw first-hand how much research and fact checking went into it, not to mention the work that was needed to achieve an amazing result in the GAMSAT at the same time – very impressive. So thank you for doing a fantastic job and supporting me during the mixed bag of emotions that are associated with writing a book, opening a new restaurant and moving to a new home … love you Hansi.

To my family, Ronnie, Steffie, Georgie, Dad, Caz, Lilli, Jack and the Reids, who have made me feel so welcome in their family. You're all a bunch of bloody legends!

To my good friend and business partner Daz. It's been an amazing journey and I'm so happy you decided to poach a few eggs all those years ago. You're an absolute top bloke. Thank you for always being there.

We would both like to thank …

Jeff Bennett, Sam Reid and Chris Sorrell for being the best business partners and coolest dudes on the planet!

Hannah for doing such an amazing job with all the text and research that went into this book.

Dom (the architect ninja), Bernie, Dan, Stuart, Jonsey, Rosco, Mitch, Scotty, Paul and Sam from Moffat, Dan the meat man, Big Dan, Freckle, Col, Sarah and Jeremy from 100 Mile Table, Timmy from Milk and Honey, Astrid and Josh from Fleet, Adam and Lara from Punch and Daisy, the guys at Deus, Patagonia and Stone & Wood – thanks for making us feel so welcome in our new Byron home.

The Bread Social boys, Pauly, Sam and Tom, Jules, Jane Magnus, Katherine and the Flowers at the Farm girls, Meranda and Anneka – thanks for all the help styling Byron. Leone McRae, thanks for your help back in the day.

Lauren, Frannie, Zlata, Meridith, Chris, Josh, Marco, Max, Joel, Kate upstairs, Nick Clifford, Brian, Ian from the pharmacy, Cal and all of team Bronte – you guys are amazing! Also thanks to the beautiful Iggy's family, Byron, Ronnie and Stephie.

Ashley Kent, Ryan, Jude, Dennis, Tristan, Zane, Andrew, Gus, Zac, Mark, Ebony, Joey, Dunstan, Sam, Andy, Dave, Freddie and all of team Byron … and, of course, Tom and Emma Lane.

Shannon D, Luke P, Hongy, Jeremy 'The Truth' Strode, Mike Clift, Mitch, Greeno, Clayton, Dan P, Martin Benn, Fassy, Louis T, Ben and Elvis, Matt Wilkinson, Monty, Jordan, Phil W, Brent S, James V, Big Mike, Jemma and Berry, Neil and Byron and all the chefs and people in the food industry who massively support us.

John Sussman, Pat and Miffy, Joanna, Tez and Jill, Huckstep, Martin Boetz, Cath and Hapi.

Thanks to our incredible suppliers, farmers and producers who make all the magic: Josh, Lynette, Cass and Kirsten. Also to Lynette and Ross McDonald.

Finally, thanks to all who worked closely on the book: Marcus for his thorough recipe deciphering skills; Felicity for the recipe testing; Will Meppem and Emma Knowles for the incredible food shots; Ant Ong for the beautiful landscape shots; Kirby Armstrong for the amazing design; Brett Armstrong for the brilliant illustrations; and Tara, Mary and the Plum team for their patience and unwavering belief in us.

INDEX